INTRODUCING
ISSUES WITH
OPPOSING
VIEWPOINTS®

Divorce

Jacqueline Langwith, *Book Editor*

GREENHAVEN PRESS
A part of Gale, Cengage Learning

GALE
CENGAGE Learning·

Detroit • New York • San Francisco • New Haven, Conn • Waterville, Maine • London

Elizabeth Des Chenes, *Managing Editor*

© 2012 Greenhaven Press, a part of Gale, Cengage Learning

Articles in Greenhaven Press anthologies are often edited for length to meet page requirements. In addition, original titles of these works are changed to clearly present the main thesis and to explicitly indicate the author's opinion. Every effort is made to ensure that Greenhaven Press accurately reflects the original intent of the authors. Every effort has been made to trace the owners of copyrighted material.

Cover image © ejwhite/Shutterstock.com.

LIBRARY OF CONGRESS CATALOGING-IN-PUBLICATION DATA

Divorce / Jacqueline Langwith, book editor.
    p. cm. -- (Introducing issues with opposing viewpoints)
  Includes bibliographical references and index.
  ISBN 978-0-7377-5674-6 (hardcover)
  1. Divorce. 2. Divorce--Law and legislation. I. Langwith, Jacqueline.
  HQ814.D587 2012
  306.89--dc23

                                                                    2011043219

Printed in the United States of America
 2 3 4 5 6 7 16 15 14 13 12

Contents

Foreword

I ndulging in a wide spectrum of ideas, beliefs, and perspectives is a critical cornerstone of democracy. After all, it is often debates over differences of opinion, such as whether to legalize abortion, how to treat prisoners, or when to enact the death penalty, that shape our society and drive it forward. Such diversity of thought is frequently regarded as the hallmark of a healthy and civilized culture. As the Reverend Clifford Schutjer of the First Congregational Church in Mansfield, Ohio, declared in a 2001 sermon, "Surrounding oneself with only like-minded people, restricting what we listen to or read only to what we find agreeable is irresponsible. Refusing to entertain doubts once we make up our minds is a subtle but deadly form of arrogance." With this advice in mind, Introducing Issues with Opposing Viewpoints books aim to open readers' minds to the critically divergent views that comprise our world's most important debates.

Introducing Issues with Opposing Viewpoints simplifies for students the enormous and often overwhelming mass of material now available via print and electronic media. Collected in every volume is an array of opinions that captures the essence of a particular controversy or topic. Introducing Issues with Opposing Viewpoints books embody the spirit of nineteenth-century journalist Charles A. Dana's axiom: "Fight for your opinions, but do not believe that they contain the whole truth, or the only truth." Absorbing such contrasting opinions teaches students to analyze the strength of an argument and compare it to its opposition. From this process readers can inform and strengthen their own opinions, or be exposed to new information that will change their minds. Introducing Issues with Opposing Viewpoints is a mosaic of different voices. The authors are statesmen, pundits, academics, journalists, corporations, and ordinary people who have felt compelled to share their experiences and ideas in a public forum. Their words have been collected from newspapers, journals, books, speeches, interviews, and the Internet, the fastest growing body of opinionated material in the world.

Introducing Issues with Opposing Viewpoints shares many of the well-known features of its critically acclaimed parent series, Opposing Viewpoints. The articles are presented in a pro/con format, allowing readers to absorb divergent perspectives side by side. Active reading questions preface each viewpoint, requiring the student to approach the material thoughtfully and carefully. Useful charts, graphs, and cartoons supplement each article. A thorough introduction provides readers with crucial background on an issue. An annotated bibliography points the reader toward articles, books, and websites that contain additional information on the topic. An appendix of organizations to contact contains a wide variety of charities, nonprofit organizations, political groups, and private enterprises that each hold a position on the issue at hand. Finally, a comprehensive index allows readers to locate content quickly and efficiently.

Introducing Issues with Opposing Viewpoints is also significantly different from Opposing Viewpoints. As the series title implies, its presentation will help introduce students to the concept of opposing viewpoints and learn to use this material to aid in critical writing and debate. The series' four-color, accessible format makes the books attractive and inviting to readers of all levels. In addition, each viewpoint has been carefully edited to maximize a reader's understanding of the content. Short but thorough viewpoints capture the essence of an argument. A substantial, thought-provoking essay question placed at the end of each viewpoint asks the student to further investigate the issues raised in the viewpoint, compare and contrast two authors' arguments, or consider how one might go about forming an opinion on the topic at hand. Each viewpoint contains sidebars that include at-a-glance information and handy statistics. A Facts About section located in the back of the book further supplies students with relevant facts and figures.

Following in the tradition of the Opposing Viewpoints series, Greenhaven Press continues to provide readers with invaluable exposure to the controversial issues that shape our world. As John Stuart Mill once wrote: "The only way in which a human being can make some approach to knowing the whole of a subject is by hearing what can be said about it by persons of every variety of opinion and studying all modes in which it can be looked at by every character of mind. No wise man ever acquired his wisdom in any mode but this." It is to this principle that Introducing Issues with Opposing Viewpoints books are dedicated.

Introduction

"When business is good, marriage and divorce rates go up. When business is bad, they go down."

—Samuel A. Stouffer and Lyle M. Spencer,
Annals of the American Academy of Political and Social Science, November 1936

D ivorce is expensive. Costs for divorce vary considerably in the United States, depending on location, whether children are involved, and the number of assets such as bank accounts, homes, and cars that need to be divvied up. According to an article from Divorce360.com, "The legal costs of an average divorce could range from $2,500 to $10,000. A contested divorce, however, can cost up to $100,000 in legal fees alone, if several large assets and children are involved."[1] Those are just the costs to get divorced. But there are costs afterward as well. For instance, married couples generally share one home, and possibly a single car. After a divorce each person needs to shoulder their own housing and transportation costs. Additional expenses are incurred when child custody is shared as children must be transported between parents. Given the costs of divorce it is not surprising to learn that a couple's decision to divorce is influenced by the economy. Generally, as the two scholars quoted above noted back in 1936, American divorce rates decrease during challenging economic times and increase when the economy is doing better.

The connection between divorce rates, as well as marriage rates, and the economy is strong. According to a 2009 article written by Alex Roberts of the Institute for American Values, researchers have studied the effects of economic conditions on marriage and divorce going back to the nineteenth century. Roberts says that "almost without exception this body of research points to one conclusion: Both marriage and divorce rates tend to fall when the economy heads south and then rise when good times return."[2]

This trend was exemplified during the Great Depression, the worst economic crisis the country has experienced. A government report from the 1970s, which looked at marriage and divorce statistics in the United States from 1867 to 1967, revealed that the divorce rate in 1932, when the Depression was in full swing, reached a low of 7.9 divorces per thousand married couples, down from 12.0 per thousand marriages in 1920.[3]

During the economic difficulties at the end of the first decade of the twenty-first century, divorce rates also dropped. What some economists have labeled the Great Recession officially began in December 2007 and lasted until June 2009. According to the Economic Policy Institute, the US labor market lost 8.4 million jobs during this time. This job loss was associated with a drop in the income and wealth of American families and a rise in the number of families in poverty. According to the annual report on marriage and divorce published by the University of Virginia's National Marriage Project, divorce rates dropped from 17.5 divorces per thousand married women in 2007 to 16.9 and 16.4 divorces per thousand married women in 2008 and 2009, respectively. Marriage rates also declined during the Great Recession; however, they had already been on a downward trend.

Some sociologists think that divorce rates decrease during tough economic times because marriages become stronger. In addition to influencing marriage and divorce rates, economic downturns have many other cultural and social impacts, sociologists have found. Among these impacts is a tendency to become more thrifty. According to Bradford W. Wilcox, director of the National Marriage Project, being thrifty can solidify a marriage. Bradford says that thrifty couples tend to spend more time together, such as at family meals, and they save their money. Writing in the *Wall Street Journal* on December 11, 2009, Wilcox asserts that couples with savings accounts and other financial assets are less likely to divorce than are free-spending couples. Wilcox also contends that divorce rates are lower during economic downturns because couples faced with difficulties often rally around each other and become closer. Wilcox writes in 2009, "Americans are rediscovering the power that family ties have to carry them—financially, socially and emotionally—through tough times."[4]

Not everyone believes tough times strengthen marriages, however. Some sociologists think that tough times weaken marriages and that couples just delay divorcing until they can afford it. Andrew J. Cherlin, a professor of sociology at Johns Hopkins University is in this group. Cherlin believes that as soon as the US economy recovers and couples can afford to separate themselves from each other, the divorce rate in America will go up. Cherlin uses statistics from the Great Depression to support his contention. He argues that the pent-up demand for divorces during the Great Depression caused the divorce rate to increase such that by the 1940s the American divorce rate was higher than before the Depression. Writing in the *New York Times* on May 28, 2009, Cherlin maintains that "the Depression destroyed the inner life of many married couples, but it was years before they could afford to file for divorce. Today's economic slump could well generate a similar backlog of couples whose relationships have been irreparably ruined. So it is only when the economy is healthy again that we will begin to see just how many fractured families have been created."[5]

Divorce is a signal characteristic of the American culture and an issue that people typically have strong feelings about. In *Introducing Issues with Opposing Viewpoints: Divorce*, sociologists, religious leaders, feminists, and commentators debate whether there is a divorce epidemic in America, what the effects of divorce are, and what types of laws should govern divorce.

Notes

1. Casey Clark-Ney, "What Does It Really Cost to Get Divorced?," Divorce360.com, July 2, 2008. www.divorce360.com/divorce -articles/finance/costs/how-much-does-divorce-ost.aspx?artid=979.
2. Alex Roberts, "Marriage and the Great Recession," *The State of Our Unions*, 2009. http://stateofourunions.or6/2009/marriage _and_the_recession.php.
3. US Department of Health, Education, and Welfare, "100 Years of Marriage and Divorce Statistics, United States, 1867–1967," December 1973. www.cdc.gov/nchs/data/series/sr_21/sr21_024.pdf.
4. Bradford W. Wilcox, "Can the Depression Save Marriage?," *Wall Street Journal*, December 11, 2009. http://online.wsi.com/article /SB10001424052748703558004574584042851448128.html.
5. Andrew J. Cherlin, "Marriage with Bankruptcy," *New York Times*, May 28, 2009. www.nytimes.com/2009/05/29/opinion/29cherlin .html.

Chapter 1

Is Divorce Epidemic in America?

The concept of divorce is symbolized here by a goldfish changing partners. The splintering of a family is a sad and stressful time for couples and their children.

Divorce Is Epidemic in America

Shmuley Boteach

In the following viewpoint, Shmuley Boteach argues that divorce is a cancer in America and the greatest family values issue facing the country. Boteach says that divorce scars men, women, and children. Those who believe in family values should focus more attention on preventing divorce than on opposing gay marriage or abortion, he says. According to Boteach, the government should provide incentives for couples to participate in marriage counseling, since this is the most straightforward way to prevent divorce.

Boteach is an American Orthodox rabbi and author. His TV program, *Shalom in the Home,* ran for two seasons on The Learning Channel (TLC).

"Divorce is epidemic in America."

AS YOU READ, CONSIDER THE FOLLOWING QUESTIONS:
1. What does Boteach think is the connection between abortion and the American divorce rate?
2. What does the author say is the reason that most families agree to appear to be on his TV show?
3. How old was Boteach when his parents divorced?

In the presidential campaign currently under way [in 2008], we hear a lot about Iraq, fighting terror, abortion, and even how many of the candidates believe in evolution. What we don't hear is anything about America's foremost national tragedy and greatest challenge: divorce. Divorce is epidemic in America. The often-cited 50 percent divorce rate is one of those statistics which can be easily and empirically verified. About half the people I know are divorced and the same would be true of the acquaintances of most other Americans. This is becoming a country of broken homes, broken families and broken children. It is a nation where kids are pawns in ugly divorce disputes and where marital passion is expressed in the divorce courts rather than in the bedroom. No child should have to grow up witnessing hatred rather than love expressed between parents. Divorce leaves incalculable destruction in its wake, from children raised without stability to men and women who often spend the remainder of their lives alone. Even more tragic is the subterfuge by which family values in America has come to mean opposing gay marriage and abortion. Even if gays never married, that would not lessen the heterosexual divorce rate, which skyrocketed well before the advent of gay rights. And divorce rates in America are unconnected to a woman's choice to have an abortion, since the vast majority of people divorcing in America are couples with children.

Incentivizing Marriage Counseling

What is needed is a national consensus on the principal family values issue of our time, namely, reducing the astronomical American divorce rate. Also needed is a bold presidential candidate who will commit, as a central plank of his or her platform, to halving the American divorce rate over the next 10 years. It is absolutely in our power to bring the divorce rate dramatically down; not by restigmatizing divorce—it is pointless to humiliate people—but in giving

According to the author, the current US divorce rate has reached epidemic proportions, with 50 percent of all marriages ending in divorce.

troubled couples the tools they need to make their marriages work and overcome crises. One of the most straightforward ways of doing so would be to grant a tax break for any money spent on marital counseling, so couples can afford the marital counseling they need. This tax break would be offered with a national registry of professional marital therapists to whom couples can turn.

It would be even better if we could get marital counseling covered by insurance companies. But I recognize that the resistance to such an idea would be ferocious, mostly from the insurance companies, whereas making marital counseling a tax deduction merely requires sufficient political will. I am often asked why families agree to appear on *Shalom in the Home* [the author's TV program on TLC]. After all, who would want to air their dirty laundry in public? It must be that they want to be on TV, right? I explain that this is rarely the case. The vast majority of families apply to be on our show because they are desperate for help and they don't know where to turn. If it is a troubled marriage, sometimes they cannot afford proper counseling or, if they can, they don't know which counselor they can trust. Enter

States with Highest and Lowest Divorce Rates* in 2009

Number of Divorces per 1,000 population

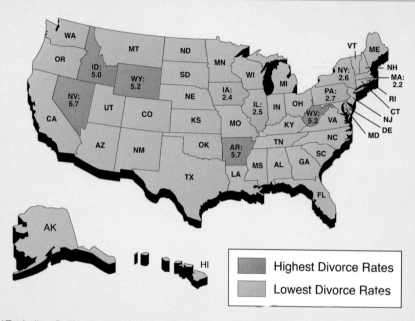

WA
OR
ID: 5.0
MT
ND
MN
SD
WY: 5.2
NE
IA: 2.4
WI
MI
NY: 2.6
VT
ME
NH
MA: 2.2
NV: 6.7
UT
CO
KS
IL: 2.5
IN
OH
PA: 2.7
WV: 5.2
VA
RI
CT
NJ
DE
CA
AZ
NM
OK
MO
AR: 5.7
TN
KY
NC
MD
TX
LA
MS
AL
GA
SC
FL
AK
HI

Highest Divorce Rates
Lowest Divorce Rates

*Excluding California, Georgia, Hawaii, Indiana, Louisiana, and Minnesota.

Taken from: US Centers For Disease Control and Prevention. National Center for Health Statistics, National Vital Statistics System.

a guy on TV whom they watch and whose philosophy they embrace. Every week I receive hundreds of emails from couples whose marriage is in crisis. They want me to counsel them in person, by phone or by email. They have few places to turn. For many of these families the availability of a trusted counselor at an affordable rate would make the difference between marriage and divorce. I have personally witnessed how just a few counseling sessions can help a couple identify the real issues destroying their relationship and, more importantly, give them the inspiration to implement a cure.

But the cost of marital counseling is outside the reach of many couples, especially if they need to go twice weekly for several months. Added to this is a reluctance on the part of couples—especially husbands—who don't believe that counseling will bring any major improvements. Hence the incentive of making the cost of counseling tax deductible could be the difference between pursuing it and not.

Creating a Loving, Compassionate Nation

Charitable contributions in nearly every country are tax deductible, as they should be, since they create benevolent nations with healthy non-profits who look after the most vulnerable elements of society, often doing a far better job than governments can do. But doesn't charity begin at home? Can we really create nations who believe in love, compassion and giving when most Western countries today are comprised of children half of whom have rarely witnessed that love and compassion at home? Can we not agree that rescuing the American family from terminal decline is the foremost national emergency of our time?

My parents divorced when I was a boy of eight, and it scarred me for life. And today, as I sit with so many married couples whose marriage is on the brink, my mind often wanders to that fateful time, more than 30 years ago, when my parents' marriage was unraveling. I ask myself whether something as straightforward as a sympathetic and wise counselor could have prevented the split that snuffed out so much of the happiness of my youth. The answer to that question will never be known. But what is certain is that couples talking out their problems leads to real and genuine healing. And it's time the leaders of our country and the politicians who claim to represent family values addressed how much of a cancer divorce is in the life of a nation, and started taking active remedies to cure it.

EVALUATING THE AUTHOR'S ARGUMENTS:

What evidence does Boteach use to support his contention that divorce is epidemic in America? Do you agree with this interpretation of the evidence? Why, or why not? What level of divorce rate would you label as an epidemic? Why?

Divorce Is Not Epidemic in America

"If divorce is an epidemic in America and half of all marriages fail, how come I so rarely meet other divorced parents?"

Kathleen Deveny

In the following viewpoint, Kathleen Deveny asserts that, contrary to common belief, divorce is not rampant in America. According to Deveny, the statistic indicating that 50 percent of marriages end in divorce is misleading because it compares marriages in a given year to divorces in the same year. According to Deveny, over the past two dozen years or so, the divorce rate has actually been decreasing.

Deveny is a reporter who has written for the *Wall Street Journal, Newsweek,* and the *Fiscal Times.*

AS YOU READ, CONSIDER THE FOLLOWING QUESTIONS:

1. According to Deveny, the oft-repeated statistic that one in two marriages ends in divorce is based on what?
2. The average divorce affected how many children in 1968, according to Deveny?
3. According to Betsey Stevenson and Justin Wolfers, as cited by the author, divorce rates are lowest among what group?

It's become a rite of each school year, a masochistic little ritual that I can't resist. As soon as my daughter's school sends out the parent directory, I open it immediately. I may glance at the teacher photos, but I'm really looking for divorced families. We're easy to spot: those painfully obvious entries with two addresses listed next to the student's name. This year, we are the only one in my daughter's class. It's not that I'd wish this on any family. But if

In 2005 the annual marriage rate was 7.5 per 1,000 people and the divorce rate 3.6 per 1,000, according to the National Center for Health Statistics.

divorce is an epidemic in America and half of all marriages fail, how come I so rarely meet other divorced parents? Have I landed in an episode of "Mad Men"?

The mystery apparently extends beyond my Brooklyn neighborhood. "The 50 percent thing doesn't seem to be my reality," says Debbie Zeitman, 47, a divorced mom who lives with her 15-year-old son in Venice, Calif. "I'm surprised by how relatively uncommon it seems to be." Dorothy Lloyd, the divorced mother of an 11-year-old girl in Highland Park, Ill., says most families where she lives are "more of the traditional kind, both parents at home."

This Does Not Feel Like a Crisis

We're not imagining things. The number of families in our position— thankfully—is much smaller than you might think. Only 10 percent of the nation's children were living with a divorced parent in 2004, according to my calculation using the most current available U.S. Census data. That doesn't include kids living with parents who have remarried, or parents who have never married. But it doesn't feel like a national crisis, either.

That's partly because the divorce rate is dropping—and has been for some 25 years. The oft-repeated statistic that one in two marriages ends up in divorce isn't exactly right. It's based on the annual marriage rate per 1,000 people, compared with the annual divorce rate. In 2005, the marriage rate was 7.5 per 1,000 people, while the divorce rate was 3.6 per 1,000, according to the National Center for Health Statistics. But since the people who get married in any given year usually are not the same people who get divorced (OK, maybe a few), the statistic isn't very meaningful. Even if you look at divorces among married couples, the rate has declined from a peak of 22.8 divorces per 1,000 in 1979 to 16.7 divorces in 2005.

> **FAST FACT**
>
> According to the US Census Bureau's American Community Survey, in 2008 the average marriage rate for men fifteen years and older was 19.6 per 1,000, while the average divorce rate was 9.9 per 1,000.

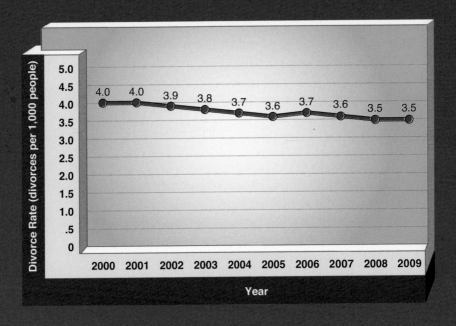

US Divorce Rates Falling

Divorce Rate (divorces per 1,000 people)

Year	Rate
2000	4.0
2001	4.0
2002	3.9
2003	3.8
2004	3.7
2005	3.6
2006	3.7
2007	3.6
2008	3.5
2009	3.5

Taken from: US Centers for Disease Control and Prevention, National Center for Health Statistics. National Vital Statistics System.

Thanks to later marriages, smaller families, longer life expectancy and the fact that unhappy couples tend to divorce faster than they used to, the number of children affected by each divorce is also shrinking. In 1968, the average divorce affected 1.34 kids, according to Betsey Stevenson and Justin Wolfers, both assistant professors at the University of Pennsylvania's Wharton School. By 1995, that number was 0.91, about the same level as 1950. And in general, divorce rates are lowest among those with a college degree, according to Stevenson. She thinks that may be because educated women tend to marry later, and the older you are when you get married, the more durable your marriage seems to be.

"You're simply running in the wrong crowd," says Stephanie Coontz, a professor of history and family studies at The Evergreen State College in Olympia, Wash. Small comfort. While not all divorced parents feel this way, I worry that people will view my daughter differently. "It's a new kind of stigma, masquerading as sympathy," says Coontz. She sees it even with people like physicians and social workers who are trained to deal with children. People have lowered expectations for children of divorce and are more likely to anticipate problems, all of which can be a self-fulfilling prophecy. No wonder I hate those parent directories.

EVALUATING THE AUTHOR'S ARGUMENTS:

Identify the anecdotal and the statistical evidence used by Deveny to support her viewpoint and then comment on which type of evidence you think is more reliable and why.

Viewpoint

3

Facebook Is Increasing Divorce Rates

Richard Alleyne

"Flirtations on [Facebook] are now becoming a major factor in marriage breakdowns."

In the following viewpoint, Richard Alleyne asserts that Facebook is ruining marriages and other relationships. According to Alleyne, Facebook and other social networking sites provide temptation that is too much for some people to ignore, and Facebook flirtations often end up leading to affairs. Alleyne says that family lawyers in the United Kingdom are finding that Facebook is implicated in a significant proportion of the divorce cases they handle.

Alleyne is the science correspondent for London's *Daily Telegraph* newspaper.

AS YOU READ, CONSIDER THE FOLLOWING QUESTIONS:
1. What portion of divorce petitions filed with an online law company in the past year contained references to Facebook, according to Alleyne?
2. According to the author, what other websites besides Facebook are tempting couples to cheat on each other?
3. What was one party to a divorce charged with after the police got involved in a divorcing couple's Facebook row, according to Alleyne?

For most people, Facebook is a harmless way to keep in touch with friends and family. But flirtations on the social networking site are now becoming a major factor in marriage breakdowns. Family lawyers have revealed that the problem has become so great that almost every divorce they have dealt with in the past year has involved the website.

One expert said she had dealt with 30 cases in the last nine months and Facebook had been implicated in them all. Whilst another online law company said one in five of their divorce petitions in the past year contain references to Facebook.

Emma Patel, the head of family law at Hart Scales & Hodges Solicitors, said the site acted like a "virtual third party" in splits.

Wife 'divorced' on Facebook (http://www.telegraph.co.uk/tech nology/facebook/452563/Husband-ends-six-year-marriage-on -Facebook.html)

Top 10 gaffes on Twitter, Facebook, and Google (http://www .telegraph.co.uk/technology/facebook/7635982/Top-10-gaffes -on-Facebook-Twitter-and-Google.html)

Social networks 'failing users', says study (http://www.telegraph .co.uk/technology/news/5878857/Social-networks-failing-users -says-study.html)

"Facebook is being blamed for an increasing number of marital breakdowns, and it is quite remarkable that all the petitions that I have seen here since May have cited Facebook one way or another," she said. "Its huge popularity as well as the lure of sites like Second Life, Illicit Encounters and Friends Reunited are tempting couples to cheat on each other. Suspicious spouses have used these to spy and find evidence of flirting and even affairs, which have then led to breakups." She said that many of the divorces came after partners found "flirty messages" on the Facebook wall of their partner—and also "inappropriate suggestive chats" which spouses can see. The lawyer said that she urged all clients to "stay off" Facebook during divorce proceedings—as it could throw a spanner in the works of it going smoothly—especially if they post photos of new lovers. She said: "They feel compelled to share their feelings online, and, in some cases, they not only express their stress, but also make inflammatory accusations against their partner. Divorce is a highly-charged and emotional time, but it is vital not to turn the situation into a public slagging match, played out for everyone to see online. The situation

According to the author, flirtations on Facebook have become a major factor in the increasing divorce rate.

Social Networking Usage: Americans Top the List

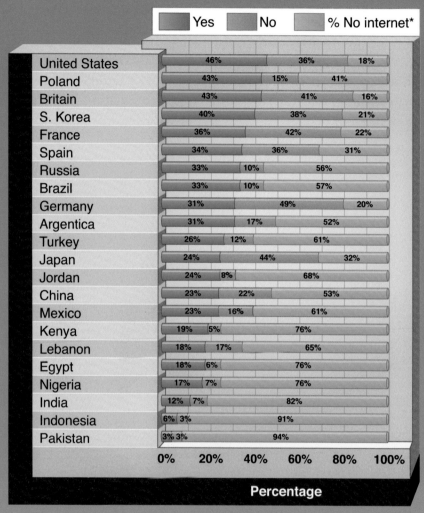

	Yes	No	% No internet*

Country	Yes	No	% No internet*
United States	46%	36%	18%
Poland	43%	15%	41%
Britain	43%	41%	16%
S. Korea	40%	38%	21%
France	36%	42%	22%
Spain	34%	36%	31%
Russia	33%	10%	56%
Brazil	33%	10%	57%
Germany	31%	49%	20%
Argentica	31%	17%	52%
Turkey	26%	12%	61%
Japan	24%	44%	32%
Jordan	24%	8%	68%
China	23%	22%	53%
Mexico	23%	16%	61%
Kenya	19%	5%	76%
Lebanon	18%	17%	65%
Egypt	18%	6%	76%
Nigeria	17%	7%	76%
India	12%	7%	82%
Indonesia	6%	3%	91%
Pakistan	3%	3%	94%

0%   20%   40%   60%   80%   100%

Percentage

*Respondents who do not use the Internet or e-mail.

Taken from: Pew Research Center. "Global Publics Embrace Social Networking." December 15, 2010.

has deteriorated so badly that we advise feuding couples to avoid these sites until their divorces are settled." The family law specialist based in Dorking, Surrey, said that one divorcing couple's rows on Facebook got so bad one party was charged with malicious communication after the police got involved.

24   **Divorce**

James Wrigley, 34, of Hackney, east London, said: "My girlfriend left me after finding out I had been sending Facebook messages to a girl at work. She got my password and read the messages and that was the end of that—four years together down the drain, but at least we hadn't got married."

Other examples include Marianna Gini, 32, a housing support worker and mother-of-one who was married for six years before she found out through Facebook that her husband Robert, 34, was having an affair. Sarah Picket, 36, a housewife from Oldham and mother-of-three was married to taxi driver Chris, also 36, for eight years, until her Facebook flirtations led to their split. She did not have an affair but her husband found flirtatious messages and the relationship ended in acrimony and jealousy.

In 2009, a 28-year-old woman, from Newquay in Cornwall, ended her marriage after discovering her husband had been having a virtual affair in cyberspace with someone he had never met.

Amy Taylor split from David Pollard after discovering he was sleeping with an escort in the game Second Life, a virtual world where players reinvent themselves.

Lauren Booth, the sister-in-law of Tony Blair, ended up causing problems in her relationship when in a fit of pique she changed the status on her Facebook profile from married to single. Miss Booth, who is the half-sister of Cherie Blair, said it was a rash decision which she changed back but not before it upset her husband.

A spokesman for Facebook said it was "tosh" that Facebook could ruin a relationship. "It is like blaming your mobile phone or your emails," he said. "Does being on Facebook force you to do something—absolutely not I would say."

EVALUATING THE AUTHOR'S ARGUMENTS:

Has Alleyne convinced you that Facebook is implicated in an increasing divorce rate? Why, or why not? Do you think Facebook could cause those in relationships to cheat on their partners? Why, or why not?

Facebook Is Not Increasing Divorce Rates

Carl Bialik

"There isn't much evidence to support the notion that social-networking sites actually cause marriages to sputter."

In the following viewpoint, Carl Bialik challenges the notion that Facebook is increasing the divorce rate. Bialik says that the "1-in-5 divorces are caused by Facebook" statistic keeps circulating in the media but is not supported by evidence. It is based, he notes, on an unscientific survey of a relatively small group of people petitioning for divorce in the United Kingdom. According to Bialik, there is a dearth of scientific research into the real causes of divorce. Carl Bialik writes a column for the *Wall Street Journal* called the Numbers Guy, which looks at the way numbers are used in the media.

AS YOU READ, CONSIDER THE FOLLOWING QUESTIONS:

1. According to Bialik, what is the relationship between divorce rates and Internet usage?
2. As cited by the author, what percentage of men and what percentage of women ascribed their divorce to mental or physical abuse in the Pennsylvania State University study that began in 1980?
3. As reported by Bialik, what results did the American Academy of Matrimonial Lawyers announce a few months after Mark Keenan issued his news release?

U pon further review, Facebook and marriage aren't incompat-
ible.
In the past two weeks, the idea that the popular social-
networking site plays a role in one in five divorces was reported by
many news organizations. This wasn't the first time that surprising
number has surfaced—it has appeared in news reports periodically
for the past year and a half [as of March 2011].

Some lawyers do say that they see Facebook and other social media
playing a role in divorce these days, as people rediscover old flames
online or strike up new relationships that lead them to stray from
their marriage vows. But lawyers and marriage researchers say there
isn't much evidence to support the notion that social-networking sites
actually cause marriages to sputter.

In fact, both the marriage and divorce rate in the U.S. have declined
as Internet usage has risen, according to the Centers for Disease Control
and Prevention's National Center for Health Statistics [NCHS]. An
annual survey of U.K. matrimonial lawyers by the accounting and con-
sulting firm Grant Thornton has found that during the Facebook era,

*Although some divorce lawyers say that social media interactions play a role in divorce—
people rediscover old flames online or begin a new relationship—others say there is not
much evidence to support this view.*

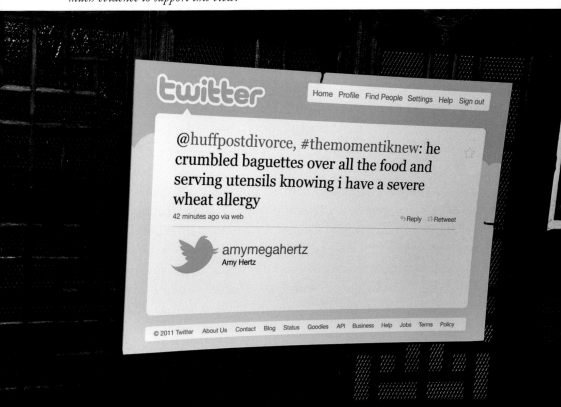

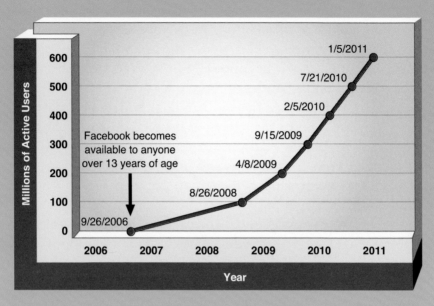

The Rise of Facebook

Taken from: Mark Zucker, Facebook Blog and Notes and Nicholas Carlson. "Goldman to Clients: Facebook Has 600 Million Users." MSNBC, January 5, 2011.

infidelity's role as the primary cause of around one-quarter of divorces has been stable. In an email, a Facebook spokesman called the notion that the site leads to divorce "ludicrous."

Knowing What Really Causes Divorce Is Difficult

Yet the 1-in-5 number has thrived in part because it helps fill a vacuum: There isn't much reliable research about what does cause divorce. Academic researchers don't even agree on how to approach the question. Some have searched for predictive demographic factors, such as age and income. Others have studied married couples' relationships to see which characteristics presage a split. Determining whether a couple is likely to break up, though, is different than identifying the actual cause.

Only a few studies have surveyed divorcees directly at the time of their divorce. One by two Pennsylvania State University researchers used as its data source 2,033 married people who had agreed to be tracked in 1980. By 1997, barely half were still reachable and amenable to interviews; of those, about one in five had gotten divorced and would discuss it. That left 208 people to be studied, a relatively small sample. And the rates of reported reasons differed between men and women. Some 9% of women ascribed their divorce to mental or physical abuse, while no men did; conversely, 9% of men said they didn't know the cause, while none of the women said this.

Even numbers on overall U.S. divorce rates are spotty. NCHS reclassified its divorce statistics as "provisional" in 1996, reflecting budgetary constraints at the agency that hampered data collection and the lack of reporting from California and a few other states that stopped tracking divorce. The figures for 2009, for example, exclude California and five other states that together contain 21% of the U.S. population.

In 2008 the Census Bureau began asking Americans in an annual survey whether they have been divorced in the last year, which is allowing researchers to start filling in gaps in state data. But so far there aren't enough data to identify trends. "To do this kind of research requires a huge amount

> **FAST FACT**
>
> According to the Pew Research Center, the average Facebook user has 229 Facebook friends.

of persistence," says George Levinger, professor emeritus of psychology at the University of Massachusetts. Still, the widespread circulation of the supposed Facebook divorce link shows how a catchy number can take on a life of its own.

The Origin of the 1-in-5 Number

The 1-in-5 number originated with an executive at an online divorce-service provider in the U.K. Mark Keenan, managing director of Divorce-Online, which allows Britons to file uncontested divorces at low cost, had just launched the company's Facebook page and wondered what role Facebook has in precipitating divorces. After determining that the word "Facebook" appeared in 989 of the company's 5,000 or so most recent divorce petitions, he had Divorce-Online issue a news release in December 2009 stating "Facebook is bad for your marriage."

Mr. Keenan acknowledges that his company's clients aren't necessarily representative of all divorces, and he adds that his firm never claimed that Facebook actually causes 20% of divorces. "It was a very unscientific survey," Mr. Keenan says.

A few months later, the American Academy of Matrimonial Lawyers announced results of a survey of its 1,600 members, 81% of whom said they had seen an increase in cases using social-networking "evidence" in the last five years. These results weren't surprising, given Facebook's phenomenal growth. But the survey drew widespread coverage that often resuscitated the 1-in-5 divorce figure.

The confusion crested [in March 2011] when Perry Drake, senior manager of media relations for Loyola University Health System in Chicago, put together a news release touting a Loyola psychologist's expertise on relationships and social media. Finding the 1-in-5 figure online, Mr. Drake led the news release with the headline: "Don't let your marriage be among the 1 in 5 destroyed by Facebook." By the time Mr. Drake became aware of the error and alerted the news release's recipients, news articles had appeared around the world. "A little sloppiness on my part has made for a bad two weeks," says Mr. Drake.

EVALUATING THE AUTHOR'S ARGUMENTS:

After reading Bialik's viewpoint, have you changed your mind about the previous viewpoint by Richard Alleyne? Compare Bialik's use of numbers and statistics to Alleyne's. Who do you think more accurately, and who more persuasively, uses numbers and statistics? Explain.

Viewpoint
5

Divorce Is Epidemic Among Baby Boomers

Richard Schlesinger

"Baby boomers . . . [make] up the majority of all divorced people in America."

In the following viewpoint, Richard Schlesinger asserts that baby boomers, generally defined as people born between 1946 and 1964, are getting divorced by the droves. According to Schlesinger, baby boomers make up the majority of all divorced people in America. Schlesinger suggests that the sexual revolution during the 1960s and increased opportunities for women may have something to do with the epidemic baby boomer divorce rate.

Schlesinger is a correspondent for the TV program *48 Hours Mystery* and a contributor to the CBS Evening News.

AS YOU READ, CONSIDER THE FOLLOWING QUESTIONS:

1. In what year did the divorce rate hit its all-time high, and what was the rate, as reported by Schlesinger?
2. According to the author, what TV character reflected the traditional wife and mother image?
3. How much longer are the children and grandchildren of baby boomers waiting to marry, according to Schlesinger?

W endy Sales was married for 25 years, and divorced for seven years. Looking at a picture of her wedding day, she said, "I actually cried when I looked at the picture because it reminded me of a time when I was really happy and hopeful about the future and thinking that this was going to be my husband forever." Like millions of other baby boomers Sales grew up in the era of [the 1950s TV show] "Leave It To Beaver," but real life ended up more like [the acrimonious divorce drama] "Kramer Vs. Kramer." By 1979, when that film came out, the divorce rate had hit its all time high—5.3 divorces per 1,000 people.

"My wife at the time used to say I was happy being miserable," said Scott Lorber. Lorber was married for five years, and divorced for 15 years. "I thought I was happy on the outside; maybe I wasn't."

Now 35 percent of all baby boomers have been divorced and that generation makes up the majority of all divorced people in America. So what happened?

Women's Options Increased

"Life happened," Sales said. "Um, we were busy."

"There's no question that a lot of women woke up during the women's movement and said, 'Who needs this,'" [American film director and producer] Nora Ephron said. Ephron has written extensively about divorce, most notably her own. She's just written [in 2010] a new book about her life and edits a blog on the *Huffington Post* all about the D-word that once dared not speak its name. "When I was growing up, the word divorce was practically whispered," Ephron said.

The traditional wife and mother image of June Cleaver [of *Leave It to Beaver*] went out with black-and-white TV. During the sexual revolution women who had said "I do" claimed their right to say, "I'd rather not."

"I was engaged at 20, married at 21 and I had my children very soon after that," said Marianne. She was married for 30 years, and divorced for seven. "Our generation was the first, at least [for] women, that were college grads and career options were open to us that the generation previous to us didn't [have]."

"I think marriage is much harder than it looks," Ephron said.

That may be why the children and grandchildren of baby boomers are waiting longer to marry—about 4 years longer. Since 1979 the

Most baby boomers grew up watching television shows such as Leave It to Beaver *that depicted idyllic American families in which divorce was never mentioned. The sexual revolution of the 1960s brought an end to such sentimental portrayals of family life.*

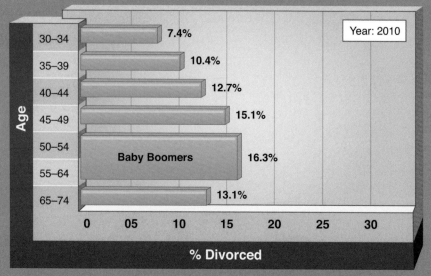

American Baby Boomers Have the Highest Rate of Divorce

Age	% Divorced
30–34	7.4%
35–39	10.4%
40–44	12.7%
45–49	15.1%
50–54	Baby Boomers 16.3%
55–64	
65–74	13.1%

Year: 2010

Taken from: US Census Bureau. Current Population Survey, 2010 Annual Social and Economic Supplement.

average age of grooms has risen from 24 to 28, and from 22 to 26 for brides. Nobody wants to inherit what turned out to be a troubling trait of an older generation.

"Nobody gets married and wants it to fail, and any way you look at it a divorce is the loss of a dream," Sales said.

EVALUATING THE AUTHOR'S ARGUMENTS:

What evidence does Schlesinger provide to support his viewpoint that baby boomers are getting divorced in large numbers? Schlesinger does not explicitly say that the women's movement had anything to do with the divorce rate, but he suggests that it did. How does he do this, and why might he simply suggest something rather than come right out and assert it?

Viewpoint

6

The Baby Boomer Divorce Epidemic Is a Myth

Christina Gregoire

"'The surge in divorced Boomers actually reflects that more divorced adults are becoming seniors.'"

In the following viewpoint, Christina Gregoire contends that there has not been a surge of baby boomer divorces. According to Gregoire, the so-called baby boomer divorce epidemic is a media hype. Gregoire says the divorce rate for boomers has been stable since the 1970s. There may be a lot of divorced boomers, she says, but they were divorced before they became senior citizens. Christina Gregoire is an artist and writer who specializes in divorce articles for the website *Suite 101*.

AS YOU READ, CONSIDER THE FOLLOWING QUESTIONS:

1. What article was the source of Gregoire's information that the boomer divorce rate has been stable since 1970?
2. What three things does the author say remarriage can affect?
3. According to Gregoire, regardless of when boomers' breakups happened, to whom should they talk?

I s there really a "graying of divorce" or is that just media hype? Divorced Baby Boomers seem to be everywhere. What about me? My friends?

If you look up anything about Baby Boomers and divorce, you will find numerous annoying articles about "the graying of divorce" and, gasp, [former US vice president] Al Gore's and Tipper's divorce. Well, what is going on? Is it an epidemic? Should we brace ourselves for the next round of divorces, worrying ourselves sick that Marilyn and [former US vice president] Dan Quayle could be next?

Relax. You are not more likely to get a divorce if you have gray hair.

Gray Divorce

Why is everyone in the media making such a fuss about "gray divorces?" According to the article "Divorce, Boomers and Financial Planning" by Lili Vasileff at divorceandfinance.org, "The real divorce rates for seniors have been nearly steady since 1970. The surge in divorced Boomers actually reflects that more divorced adults are becoming seniors."

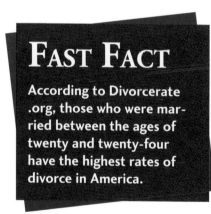

It is hard to get a handle on Baby Boomer trends by looking only at marriage and divorce statistics. Many Boomers are, indeed, divorced, but not all of those divorced men and women are single. In the last decade, the number of senior men and women who are "living together" has almost doubled. Therefore, these cohabiting people, though unmarried, are hardly single or lonely. And, these findings are not surprising. The Baby Boomers are, for better or worse, the generation that made the cohabitation trend acceptable and mainstream in the 70s.

Every couple has a different, unique story; however, the overriding reason that Boomers refrain from tying the knot (a second or third time) is their fear of financial loss. In addition, when the economy is sputtering, financial difficulties are magnified, as it is harder to replace lost income or assets.

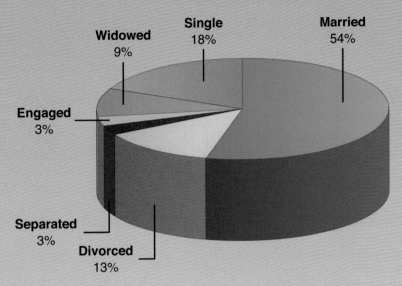

Relationship Status: Americans Forty-Five Years and Older

Widowed 9%

Single 18%

Married 54%

Engaged 3%

Separated 3%

Divorced 13%

Based on a survey of 1,670 adults in August 2009.

Taken from: Linda Fisher. "Sex, Romance, and Relationships." American Association of Retired Persons, (AARP). Washington DC, May 2010.

Remarriage can affect:

• medical insurance
• pension
• Social Security

Divorce and Medical Insurance

Here is one common way that health-insurance issues can affect remarriage statistics. A woman who remarries may lose the medical insurance she depends on from her former spouse. (Women often negotiate for health insurance during their divorces.) So, a bad medical history can thwart the possibility of remarriage for many older women. When younger couples divorce, health and healthcare coverage is less likely to be an issue when considering marriage or remarriage.

The author argues that the surge in the divorce rate for baby boomers simply reflects the fact that more divorced "boomers" are becoming seniors. Divorce rates for seniors have actually remained almost steady since 1970.

Divorce and Social Security

Although Baby Boomer women have usually worked at some point in their lives, it is quite likely that their husbands' lifetime earnings are greater than their own lifetime earnings. A woman's benefits, as an ex-spouse and divorced survivor, may be higher than the amount she would get from Social Security on her own. Women in this situation may be better off staying single than remarrying. However, there are many variables that can affect this, so women should talk to a financial planner about their specific circumstances.

Divorce and Pensions

When Baby Boomers divorce just before or during their retirement years, there are important pension scenarios that must be considered. A financial planner can help to determine the best ways to handle divorce-pension negotiations. Many older women qualify for a portion of their husbands' pensions.

The "graying" of divorce may not be a new epidemic, however many Baby Boomers have been divorced at least once in their lifetimes. Whether the break-up happened when they were in their 20s or in their 60s, there are definitely a lot of divorced Baby Boomers who should talk to financial planners about divorce, retirement, and remarriage.

EVALUATING THE AUTHOR'S ARGUMENTS:

What factual information does Gregoire use to support her viewpoint? What subjective information does she use? Which one does she depend on the most? Which do you find more convincing? Why?

The Divorce Rate Among Christians Is a Scandal

R. Albert Mohler Jr.

"The real scandal is . . . that evangelical Protestants divorce at rates at least as high as the rest of the public."

In the following viewpoint, R. Albert Mohler Jr. maintains that the acceptance of divorce in the evangelical Christian community is shameful. According to Mohler, divorce is harmful to children and families and is clearly a sin, according to the Bible; however, it does not merit much attention from the religious community in the United States. Mohler thinks churches have decided not to confront divorce because it is so common, and they are afraid of losing members. Mohler believes evangelical leaders should focus as much attention on the scandal of divorce as they do on other "family values" issues, such as abortion and gay marriage.

Mohler is the president of the Southern Baptist Theological Seminary. He is also the author of several books and a blog and frequently appears on TV to provide commentary on moral, cultural, and theological issues.

AS YOU READ, CONSIDER THE FOLLOWING QUESTIONS:
1. According to Mohler, in the most general sense, the culture war refers to what?
2. Who was the leader of the Moral Majority, a "pro-traditional family" group that was active during the 1970s and 1980s, as mentioned by the author?
3. According to Mohler, when it comes to divorce, what have evangelicals allowed to trump Scripture?

Mark A. Smith, who teaches political science at the University of Washington, pays close attention to what is now commonly called the "culture war" in America. Though the roots of this cultural conflict reach back to the 1960s, the deep divide over social and moral issues became almost impossible to deny during the late 1970s and ever since. It is now common wisdom to speak of "red" states and "blue" states and to expect familiar lines of division over questions such as abortion and homosexuality.

Divorce Absent from the Culture Wars

In the most general sense, the culture war refers to the struggle to determine laws and customs on a host of moral and political issues that separate Americans into two opposing camps, often presented as the religious right and the secular left. Though the truth is never so simple, the reality of the culture war is almost impossible to deny.

And yet, as Professor Smith surveyed the front lines of the culture war, he was surprised, not so much by the issues of hot debate and controversy, but by an issue that was obvious for its absence—divorce.

"From the standpoint of simple logic, divorce fits cleanly within the category of 'family values' and hence hypothetically could represent a driving force in the larger culture war," he notes. "If 'family values' refers to ethics and behavior that affect, well, families, then divorce obviously should qualify. Indeed, divorce seems to carry a more direct connection to the daily realities of families than do the bellwether culture war issues of abortion and homosexuality."

That logic is an indictment of evangelical failure and a monumental scandal of the evangelical conscience. When faced with this indictment, many evangelicals quickly point to the adoption of so-called "no fault" divorce laws in the 1970s. Yet, while those laws have been devastating to families (and especially to children), Smith makes a compelling case that evangelicals began their accommodation to divorce even before those laws took effect. No fault divorce laws simply reflected an acknowledgment of what had already taken place. As he explains, American evangelicals, along with other Christians, began to shift opinion on divorce when divorce became more common and when it hit close to home.

When the Christian right was organized in the 1970s and galvanized in the 1980s, the issues of abortion and homosexuality were front and center. Where was divorce? Smith documents the fact that groups such as the "pro-traditional family" Moral Majority led by the late Jerry Falwell generally failed even to mention divorce in their publications or platforms.

"During the 10 years of its existence, Falwell's organization mobilized and lobbied on many political issues, including abortion, pornography, gay rights, school prayer, the Equal Rights Amendment, and sex education in schools," he recalls. Where is divorce—a tragedy that affects far more families than the more "hot button" issues? "Divorce failed to achieve that exalted status, ranking so low on the group's agenda that books on the Moral Majority do not even give the issue an entry in the index."

Divorce Is Common in Evangelical Communities

But the real scandal is far deeper than missing listings in an index. The real scandal is the fact that evangelical Protestants divorce at rates at least as high as the rest of the public. Needless to say, this creates a significant credibility crisis when evangelicals then rise to speak in defense of marriage.

As for the question of divorce and public law, Smith traces a huge transition in the law and in the larger cultural context. In times past,

The Moral Majority organization headed by Jerry Falwell (pictured) lobbied the government on many political issues, including abortion, pornography, gay rights, and school prayer. It did not, however, address the threat of divorce to Christian "family values."

he explains, both divorce and marriage were considered matters of intense public interest. But at some point, the culture was transformed, and divorce was reclassified as a purely private matter.

Tragically, the church largely followed the lead of its members and accepted what might be called the "privatization" of divorce. Churches simply allowed a secular culture to determine that divorce is no big deal, and that it is a purely private matter.

As Smith argues, the Bible is emphatic in condemning divorce. For this reason, you would expect to find evangelical Christians demanding the inclusion of divorce on a list of central concerns and aims. But this seldom happened. Evangelical Christians rightly demanded laws that would defend the sanctity of human life. Not so for marriage. Smith explains that the inclusion of divorce on the agenda of the Christian right would have risked a massive alienation of members. In summary, evangelicals allowed culture to trump Scripture.

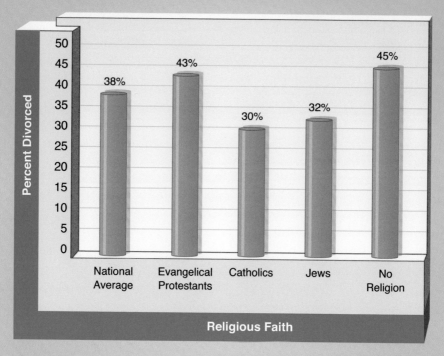

Divorce Rates for Different Religious Faiths, 1973–2006

Percent Divorced

- National Average: 38%
- Evangelical Protestants: 43%
- Catholics: 30%
- Jews: 32%
- No Religion: 45%

Religious Faith

Taken from: Mark A. Smith. "Religion, Divorce, and the Missing Culture War in America." *Political Science Quarterly,* Spring, 2010.

An even greater tragedy is the collapse of church discipline within congregations. A perceived "zone of privacy" is simply assumed by most church members, and divorce is considered only a private concern.

Professor Smith is concerned with this question as a political scientist. Why did American evangelicals surrender so quickly as divorce gathered momentum in America? We must ask this same question with even greater urgency. How did divorce, so clearly identified as a grievous sin in the Bible, become so commonplace and accepted in our midst?

Evangelicals Must Confront Divorce

The sanctity of human life is a cause that demands our priority and sacrifice. The challenge represented by the possibility (or probability) of legalized same-sex marriage demands our attention and involvement, as well.

But divorce harms many more lives than will be touched by homosexual marriage. Children are left without fathers, wives without husbands, and homes are forever broken. Fathers are separated from their children, and marriage is irreparably undermined as divorce becomes routine and accepted. Divorce is not the unpardonable sin, but it *is* sin, and it is a sin that is condemned in no uncertain terms.

Evangelical Christians are gravely concerned about the family, and this is good and necessary. But our credibility on the issue of marriage is significantly discounted by our acceptance of divorce. To our shame, the culture war is not the only place that an honest confrontation with the divorce culture is missing.

Divorce is now the scandal of the evangelical conscience.

EVALUATING THE AUTHOR'S ARGUMENTS:

What authority do you think Mohler has to write about the evangelical community? What is the primary source of information that Mohler uses to support his viewpoint? Do you think this is a reliable and trustworthy source? Explain your answers.

Viewpoint

8

Christian Divorce Rates Are Exaggerated

Glenn T. Stanton

"The divorce rate among Christians is significantly lower than the general population."

In the following viewpoint, Glenn T. Stanton contends that Christians do not divorce as often as do nonbelievers. According to Stanton, the divorce rate among committed and practicing Christians is significantly lower than the divorce rate in the general population. Additionally, he says, the divorce rate for people practicing other traditional religious faiths is lower than the rate in the general public. Stanton says couples who actively practice their religion and take their faith seriously have lower divorce rates than do nonbelievers, the general public, or people that are church members, but not religiously committed.

Stanton is the director for family formation studies at Focus on the Family, an evangelical organization based in Colorado. He is also the author of the 2011 book *Secure Daughters, Confident Sons: How Parents Guide Their Children into Authentic Masculinity and Femininity.*

Glenn T. Stanton, "First-Person: The Christian Divorce Rate Myth (What You've Heard Is Wrong)," *Baptist Press,* February 15, 2011. Reproduced by permission.

AS YOU READ, CONSIDER THE FOLLOWING QUESTIONS:
  1. According to Stanton, what is one of the most quoted statistics by Christian leaders today?
  2. What is the divorce rate for nominally attending conservative Protestants compared to secular Americans, according to the study performed by W. Bradford Wilcox, as cited by the author?
  3. What study did Professor Scott Stanley work on, according to Stanton?

"Christians divorce at roughly the same rate as the world!" It's one of the most quoted stats by Christian leaders today. And it's perhaps one of the most inaccurate.

Based on the best data available, the divorce rate among Christians is significantly lower than the general population.

Here's the truth . . .

Many people who seriously practice a traditional religious faith—be it Christian or other—have a divorce rate markedly lower than the general population.

Religious Commitment and Practice

The factor making the most difference is religious commitment and practice. Couples who regularly practice any combination of serious religious behaviors and attitudes—attend church nearly every week, read their Bibles and spiritual materials regularly; pray privately and together; generally take their faith seriously, living not as perfect disciples, but serious disciples—enjoy significantly lower divorce rates than mere church members, the general public and unbelievers.

Professor Bradley Wright, a sociologist at the University of Connecticut, explains from his analysis of people who identify as Christians but rarely attend church, that 60 percent of these have been divorced. Of those who attend church regularly, 38 percent have been divorced.

Other data from additional sociologists of family and religion suggest a significant marital stability divide between those who take their faith seriously and those who do not.

The author says that couples who actively practice their religion take their faith seriously and, consequently, have lower divorce rates than nonbelievers.

W. Bradford Wilcox, a leading sociologist at the University of Virginia and director of the National Marriage Project, finds from his own analysis that "active conservative Protestants" who regularly attend church are 35 percent less likely to divorce compared to those who have no affiliation. Nominally attending conservative Protestants are 20 percent more likely to divorce, compared to secular Americans.

Professor Scott Stanley from the University of Denver, working with an absolute all-star team of leading sociologists on the Oklahoma Marriage Study, explains that couples with a vibrant religious faith had more and higher levels of the qualities couples need to avoid divorce:

FAST FACT

Without considering other factors, couples married in a religious ceremony have a 30 percent lower risk of separation or marriage dissolution than those who married in civil or other ceremonies, according to a study of nearly three thousand American couples published in 2009.

"Whether young or old, male or female, low-income or not, those who said that they were more religious reported higher average levels of commitment to their partners, higher levels of marital satisfaction, less thinking and talking about divorce and lower levels of negative interaction. These patterns held true when controlling for such important variables as income, education, and age at first marriage."

These positive factors translated into actual lowered risk of divorce among active believers.

"Those who say they are more religious are less likely, not more, to have already experienced divorce. Likewise, those who report more frequent attendance at religious services were significantly less likely to have been divorced."

Faith Does Matter

The divorce rates of Christian believers are not identical to the general population—not even close. Being a committed, faithful believer makes a measurable difference in marriage.

Women Whose Religion Is Important Are Less Likely to Divorce

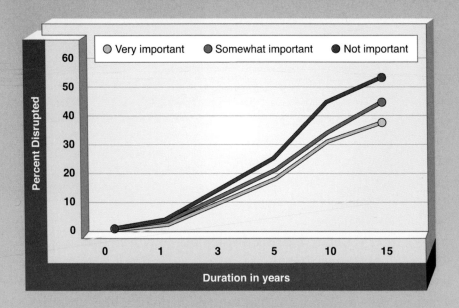

Probability that the first marriage breaks up by duration of marriage and importance of religion: United States, 1995

Taken from: M.D. Bramlett and W.D. Mosher. "Cohabitation, Marriage, Divorce, and Remarriage in the United States." *National Center for Health Statistics*, Vital and Health Statistics, July 2002.

Saying you believe something or merely belonging to a church, unsurprisingly, does little for marriage. But the more you are involved in the actual practice of your faith in real ways—through submitting yourself to a serious body of believers, learning regularly from Scripture, being in communion with God through prayer individually and with your spouse and children, and having friends and family around you who challenge you to take your marriage seriously—the greater difference this makes in strengthening both the quality and longevity of our marriages. Faith does matter and the leading sociologists of family and religion tell us so.

Chapter 2

What Are the Effects of Divorce?

The people most affected by divorce are often the children.

Divorce Harms Individuals and Society

Kevin Hassett

"Even quiet divorces can have terrible consequences both for the individuals involved and for society as a whole."

In the following viewpoint, Kevin Hassett argues that the individual and societal costs of divorce are high. According to Hassett, women and children are particularly vulnerable to the effects of divorce. Women generally suffer economically after a divorce. Divorce affects children in multiple ways. They suffer academically, mentally, and socially, and these effects are long lasting. Fixing the problem of divorce in America is daunting, contends Hassett; however, the stakes are too high for the government to ignore the issue.

Hassett is the director of economic policy studies at the American Enterprise Institute, a conservative nonpartisan organization, and is a Bloomberg News columnist.

AS YOU READ, CONSIDER THE FOLLOWING QUESTIONS:
1. What did researchers at Ohio State University, as cited by the author, find out about the wealth of women compared with that of men after a divorce?
2. According to Hassett, how did President George W. Bush's 2001 tax cuts try to eliminate marriage disincentives brought about by the tax code?
3. What is a good way to use the scientific method to discover innovative public programs that work, in the author's opinion?

The news that the messy divorce trial of Christie Brinkley and Peter Cook ended with a settlement last week came a little too late for the two parties. The ugliness of the case was best-captured by the news alert posted by the Associated Press announcing the settlement: "Christie Brinkley settles NY divorce with husband who had teen mistress, online porn habit."

Having a publicly contested divorce clearly took its toll on the unfortunate couple, but the sad fact is that even quiet divorces can have terrible consequences both for the individuals involved and for society as a whole. Indeed, a growing body of economic literature has added up the cost of divorce and the related problem of single parenthood and found them to be astonishingly large.

The sheer enormity of these costs has policy makers scratching their heads and looking for solutions. According to the U.S. Department of Health and Human Services, 48 percent of marriages in the U.S. will end in divorce if current marriage and divorce rates continue in the future. Marriage itself is less-common as well, so the traditional nuclear family—father, mother and children—now makes up fewer than 28 percent of all households. There are more households, fully 32 percent, that are made up of single individuals or those cohabitating with non-family members.

The evidence suggests that divorce has a strongly negative effect on females, in particular. Researchers at Ohio State University found that while divorce reduces a person's wealth by an average of 77 percent, men typically have 2.5 times the wealth of women after a divorce.

Toll on Children

Living in a family that is not of the traditionally nuclear variety also takes a toll on children. A thought-provoking review of the literature by economists Ron Haskins of the Brookings Institution, Sara McLanahan of the Center for Research on Child Wellbeing at Princeton University, and Elisabeth Donohue of the Woodrow Wilson School of Public and International Affairs at Princeton University, highlights the costs vividly.

Most compelling is their discussion of a 2005 study by Paul Amato: "Amato reports that if the same share of children lived with their biological parents today as did in 1980, about 300,000 fewer chil-

Women are more likely than men to suffer emotionally and financially following divorce.

dren between the ages of 12 and 18 would repeat a grade, 485,000 fewer would be suspended from school, 250,000 fewer would need psychotherapy, 210,000 fewer would be involved in violence, and 30,000 fewer would attempt suicide every year."

Understating the Cost

Since kids who have trouble in school are more likely to have trouble thereafter, these numbers understate the true cost to society of the decline of marriage.

Is there anything Washington can do to help revive the traditional environment that serves children so well? You can hardly say policy makers haven't tried. Over the past decade or so, a number of steps have been taken.

The 1996 welfare reform set a national goal of encouraging the "formation and maintenance of two-parent families" and reducing the number of out-of-wedlock births. This translated into TANF—Temporary Assistance for Needy Families—block grants for states, designated for "promoting healthy marriages."

Ad Campaigns

President George W. Bush expanded these efforts in 2002 with the Healthy Marriage Initiative. The program provides $100 million per year in state grants designed to "help couples, who have chosen marriage for themselves gain greater access to marriage-education services, where they can acquire the skills and knowledge necessary to form and sustain a healthy marriage." The funding is put toward advertising campaigns on the value of marriage, public school educational programs, and a research initiative on marriage, among other things. In addition, Bush's 2001 tax cuts also tried to eliminate any marriage disincentives brought about through the tax code. The law relieved married couples in lower tax brackets from the "marriage penalty" by increasing their standard deduction to twice that of singles. These efforts, though, have hardly made a dent in the problem. That's evident both from the macroeconomic trends, which continue to worsen, and from the scientific literature. Summarizing what we know, Haskins, McLanahan and Donohue write that "the evidence that pro-marriage programs will produce benefits is thin."

So what should we do? First, both political parties have to recognize that discussion of the benefits of marriage can't dissolve into intolerance. The benefits of higher marriage rates are great. An effective program would be a godsend for children. Crafted well, it should be uncontroversial.

> **FAST FACT**
>
> According to a 2008 study by an economist from Georgia College & State University, the cost to US taxpayers of high rates of divorce and unmarried childbearing is at least $112 billion each year.

Costs of Family Fragmentation to States

Taxpayer Costs of Public Programs Affected by High Divorce and Unwed Childbearing

WA

MT

ND

MN

NY: $3.7 Billion

VT

ME

OR

ID

WY

SD

WI

MI

NH

MA

NV: $0.2 Billion

UT

CO

NE

IA

IL

IN

OH

PA

RI

CT

CA $4.8 Billion

KS

MO $0.7 Billion

KY

WV

VA

NJ

DE

AZ

NM

OK

AR

TN

NC

MD

TX $3 Billion

LA

MS

AL $0.5 Billion

GA

SC

FL $1.9 Billion

AK

HI

Taken from: Benjamin Scafidi. "The Taxpayer Costs of Divorce and Unwed Childbearing." *Institute for American Values*, 2008.

Admit Failure

Second, we need to acknowledge that our efforts to address the problem so far have been inadequate. This may be because the problem is insurmountable; it also might be because programs in place, such as those that provide counseling, have yet to stumble upon a magic formula.

Even a devout libertarian would have to admit that the stakes are too high to ignore. Accordingly, Congress should follow the advice of Haskins, McLanahan and Donohue and commit to using the scientific method to discover innovative public programs that work. A good way to do this would be to provide ample research grants for pilot programs designed to encourage family formation, and to consider relying on faith-based initiatives in this area as well. Even the best programs will provide little help to couples with conflicts as serious as those facing Brinkley and Cook, but even minor progress in this area could provide ample social benefits.

EVALUATING THE AUTHOR'S ARGUMENTS:

What do you think is Hassett's primary purpose in writing this essay? Do you think he is trying to convince you that the costs of divorce are high or to convince you that government programs are needed? Has he convinced you to accept either of these contentions? Why, or why not?

Viewpoint

2

Divorce Hits Low-Income People Especially Hard

"The fallout of America's retreat from marriage has hit poor and working-class communities especially hard."

W. Bradford Wilcox

In the following viewpoint, W. Bradford Wilcox contends that divorce affects poor, working-class, and undereducated Americans and their children more than it does wealthier and college-educated Americans. Wilcox contends that all Americans were affected by the divorce revolution of the 1960s and 1970s; however, while the divorce rate has stabilized and marital success has increased among wealthier Americans, he argues that the trends have gone in the opposite direction for those in lower-income communities. Wilcox attributes this "divorce divide" to changing cultural and economic views of divorce and marriage in working-class and poor communities. W. Bradford Wilcox is a sociologist and the director of the National Marriage Project at the University of Virginia.

W. Bradford Wilcox, "The Evolution of Divorce." *National Affairs,* Fall 2009. All rights reserved. Reproduced by permission.

C learly, the divorce revolution of the 1960s and '70s left a poisonous legacy. But what has happened since? Where do we stand today on the question of marriage and divorce? A survey of the landscape presents a decidedly mixed portrait of contemporary married life in America.

Divorce Stabilization

The good news is that, on the whole, divorce has declined since 1980 and marital happiness has largely stabilized. The divorce rate fell from a historic high of 22.6 divorces per 1,000 married women in 1980 to 17.5 in 2007. In real terms, this means that slightly more than 40% of contemporary first marriages are likely to end in divorce, down from approximately 50% in 1980. Perhaps even more important, recent declines in divorce suggest that a clear majority of children who are now born to married couples will grow up with their married mothers and fathers.

Similarly, the decline in marital happiness associated with the tidal wave of divorce in the 1960s and '70s essentially stopped more than two decades ago. Men's marital happiness hovered around 63% from the early 1980s to the mid-2000s, while women's marital happiness fell just a bit, from 62% in the early 1980s to 60% in the mid-2000s.

This good news can be explained largely by three key factors. First, the age at first marriage has risen. In 1970, the median age of marriage was 20.8 for women and 23.2 for men; in 2007, it was 25.6 for women and 27.5 for men. This means that fewer Americans are marrying when they are too immature to forge successful marriages.

(It is true that some of the increase in age at first marriage is linked to cohabitation, but not the bulk of it.)

Second, the views of academic and professional experts about divorce and family breakdown have changed significantly in recent decades. Social-science data about the consequences of divorce have moved many scholars across the political spectrum to warn against continuing the divorce revolution, and to argue that intact families are essential, especially to the well-being of children. Here is a characteristic example, from a recent publication by a group of scholars at the Brookings Institution and Princeton University:

> Marriage provides benefits both to children and to society. Although it was once possible to believe that the nation's high rates of divorce, cohabitation, and nonmarital childbearing represented little more than lifestyle alternatives brought about by the freedom to pursue individual self-fulfillment, many analysts now believe that these individual choices can be damaging to the children who have no say in them and to the society that enables them.

Although certainly not all scholars, therapists, policymakers, and journalists would agree that contemporary levels of divorce and family breakdown are cause for worry, a much larger share of them expresses concern about the health of marriage in America—and about America's high level of divorce—than did so in the 1970s. These views seep into the popular consciousness and influence behavior— just as they did in the 1960s and '70s, when academic and professional experts carried the banner of the divorce revolution.

A Divorce and Marriage Divide

A third reason for the stabilization in divorce rates and marital happiness is not so heartening. Put simply, marriage is increasingly the preserve of the highly educated and the middle and upper classes. Fewer working-class and poor Americans are marrying nowadays in part because marriage is seen increasingly as a sort of status symbol: a sign that a couple has arrived both emotionally and financially, or is at least within range of the American Dream. This means that those who do marry today are more likely to start out enjoying the money, education, job security, and social skills that increase the probability of long-term marital success.

And this is where the bad news comes in. When it comes to divorce *and* marriage, America is increasingly divided along class and educational lines. Even as divorce in general has declined since the 1970s, what sociologist Steven Martin calls a "divorce divide" has also been growing between those with college degrees and those without (a distinction that also often translates to differences in income). The figures are quite striking: College-educated Americans have seen their divorce rates drop by about 30% since the early 1980s, whereas Americans without college degrees have seen their divorce rates increase by about 6%. Just under a quarter of college-educated couples who married in the early 1970s divorced in their first ten years of marriage, compared to 34% of their less-educated peers. Twenty years later, only 17% of college-educated couples who married in the early 1990s divorced in their first ten years of marriage; 36% of less-educated couples who married in the early 1990s, however, divorced sometime in their first decade of marriage.

This growing divorce divide means that college-educated married couples are now about half as likely to divorce as their less-educated peers. Well-educated spouses who come from intact families, who enjoy annual incomes over $60,000, and who conceive their first child in wedlock—as many college-educated couples do—have exceedingly low rates of divorce.

Similar trends can be observed in measures of marital quality. For instance, if we look at married couples aged 18–60, 72% of spouses who were both college-educated and 65% of spouses who were both less-educated reported that they were "very happy" in their marriages in the 1970s, according to the General Social Survey [a government survey of Americans begun in 1972]. In the 2000s, marital happiness remained high among college-educated spouses, as 70% continued to report that they were "very happy" in their marriages. But marital happiness fell among less-educated spouses: Only 56% reported that they were "very happy" in their marriages in the 2000s.

These trends are mirrored in American illegitimacy statistics. Although one would never guess as much from the regular *New York Times* features on successful single women having children, non-marital childbearing is quite rare among college-educated women.

According to a 2007 Child Trends study, only 7% of mothers with a college degree had a child outside of marriage, compared to more than 50% of mothers who had not gone to college.

So why are marriage and traditional child-rearing making a modest comeback in the upper reaches of society while they continue to unravel among those with less money and less education? Both cultural and economic forces are at work, each helping to widen the divorce and marriage divide in America.

Changing Views

First, while it was once the case that working-class and poor Americans held more conservative views of divorce than their middle- and upper-class peers, this is no longer so. For instance, a 2004 National Fatherhood Initiative poll of American adults aged 18–60 found that 52% of college-educated Americans endorsed the norm that in the "absence of violence and extreme conflict, parents who have an unsatisfactory marriage should stay together until their children are grown." But only 35% of less-educated Americans surveyed endorsed the same viewpoint.

Research by noted sociologists shows that lower-income couples are more likely to struggle with conflict, infidelity, substance abuse, and homelessness than those in higher-income brackets.

Likewise, according to my analysis of the General Social Survey, in the 1970s only 36% of college-educated Americans thought divorce should be "more difficult to obtain than it is now," compared to 46% of less-educated Americans. By the 2000s, 49% of college-educated Americans thought divorce laws should be tightened, compared to 48% of less-educated Americans. Views of marriage have been growing more conservative among elites, but not among the poor and the less educated.

Second, the changing cultural meaning of marriage has also made it less necessary and less attractive to working-class and poor Americans. Prior to the 1960s, when the older, institutional model of marriage dominated popular consciousness, marriage was the only legitimate venue for having sex, bearing and raising children, and enjoying an intimate relationship. Moreover, Americans generally saw marriage as an institution that was about many more goods than a high-quality emotional relationship. Therefore, it made sense for all men and women—regardless of socioeconomic status—to get and stay married.

The Soul-Mate Marriage Model

Yet now that the institutional model has lost its hold over the lives of American adults, sex, children, and intimacy can be had outside of marriage. All that remains unique to marriage today is the prospect of that high-quality emotional bond—the soul-mate model. As a result, marriage is now disproportionately appealing to wealthier, better-educated couples, because less-educated, less-wealthy couples often do not have the emotional, social, and financial resources to enjoy a high-quality soul-mate marriage.

The qualitative research of sociologists Kathryn Edin and Maria Kefalas, for instance, shows that lower-income couples are much more likely to struggle with conflict, infidelity, and substance abuse than their higher-income peers, especially as the economic position of working-class men has grown more precarious since the 1970s. Because of shifts away from industrial employment and toward service occupations, real wages and employment rates have dropped markedly for working-class men, but not for college-educated men. For instance, from 1973 to 2007, real wages of men with a college degree rose 18%; by contrast, the wages of high-school-educated men fell 11%. Likewise, in 1970, 96% of men aged 25–64 with high-school degrees or with college degrees were employed. By 2003, employment had fallen only to 93% for college-educated men of working age. But for working-aged men with only high-school degrees, labor-force participation had fallen to 84%, according to research by economist Francine Blau. These trends indicate that less-educated men have, in economic terms, become much less attractive as providers for their female peers than have college-educated men.

In other words, the soul-mate model of marriage does not extend equal marital opportunities. It therefore makes sense that fewer poor Americans would take on the responsibilities of modern married life, knowing that they are unlikely to reap its rewards.

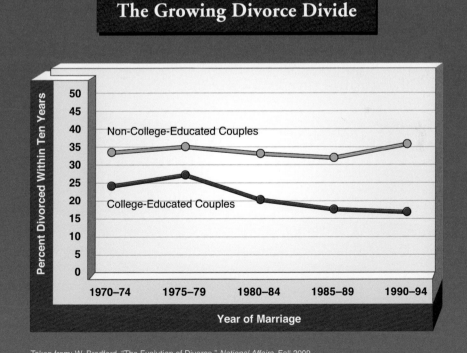

The Growing Divorce Divide

Non-College-Educated Couples

College-Educated Couples

Percent Divorced Within Ten Years

1970–74   1975–79   1980–84   1985–89   1990–94

Year of Marriage

Taken from: W. Bradford. "The Evolution of Divorce." *National Affairs*, Fall 2009.

A Host of Other Problems

The emergence of the divorce and marriage divide in America exacerbates a host of other social problems. The breakdown of marriage in working-class and poor communities has played a major role in fueling poverty and inequality, for instance. Isabel Sawhill at the Brookings Institution has concluded that virtually all of the increase in child poverty in the United States since the 1970s can be attributed to family breakdown. Meanwhile, the dissolution of marriage in working-class and poor communities has also fueled the growth of government, as federal, state, and local governments spend more money on police, prisons, welfare, and court costs, trying to pick up the pieces of broken families. Economist Ben Scafidi recently found that the public costs of family breakdown exceed $112 billion a year.

Moreover, children in single-parent homes are more likely to be exposed to Hollywood's warped vision of sex, relationships, and family life. For instance, a study by the Kaiser Family Foundation found that children in single-parent homes devote almost 45 minutes more per day to watching television than children in two-parent homes. Given the distorted nature of the popular culture's family-related messages, and the unorthodox family relationships of celebrity role models, this means that children in single-parent families are even less likely to develop a healthy understanding of marriage and family life—and are therefore less likely to have a positive vision of their own marital future.

Thus, the fallout of America's retreat from marriage has hit poor and working-class communities especially hard, with children on the lower end of the economic spectrum doubly disadvantaged by the material *and* marital circumstances of their parents.

EVALUATING THE AUTHOR'S ARGUMENTS:

What are Wilcox's credentials in writing this viewpoint? Do you think his essay is based on generalizations or specifics? Explain. Do you think he adequately supports his viewpoint that divorce especially hurts lower-income Americans? Why, or why not?

Divorce Harms Children

Nelson Acquilano

"Divorce harms children in virtually every measure."

In the following viewpoint, Nelson Acquilano asserts that divorce can have devastating long-term impacts on the lives of children. According to Acquilano, research from numerous individuals and organizations indicates that children from divorced families face a higher risk of experiencing serious difficulties in their lives, including substance abuse, academic struggles, psychiatric problems, suicide, and myriad other challenges. Acquilano contends that children of divorce never learn how to have a successful marriage, and they pass these deficiencies on to their children in a destructive cycle of divorce.

Acquilano is a social worker and the author of the 2007 book *America's Real Weapons of Mass Destruction: The Decimation of the Quality of Life in America.*

AS YOU READ, CONSIDER THE FOLLOWING QUESTIONS:

1. Why does Acquilano say that family breakup is extremely detrimental to children?
2. What acronym does the author give to the children of divorce?
3. According to Acquilano, research shows that what percentage of runaway children come from fatherless homes?

Divorce means to dissolve a marriage bond, to end a marriage. But it can also mean a curse placed upon children, an intergenerational curse upon grandchildren.

Divorce can mean tearing a beautiful family unit unwhole, incomplete, never again to be full and joyous. Divorce means never again experiencing the holidays without the feeling that someone is missing in that empty chair.

Divorce is a poorly understood phenomena in American culture. While most people agree that divorce is undesirable, few people truly

Numerous studies indicate that children of divorced families face increased risk of substance abuse, academic troubles, and psychological problems.

recognize the full degree of destruction and permanent harm it causes. New research finds that it is one of the most deleterious of the risk factors for children in any society.

Long-Term Impact

Divorce has led to the ruin of hundreds of thousands of children and adults. It destroys in a subtle way, usually in a subtle and injurious way and is much under-appreciated. Divorce is a life-transforming experience for all parties involved. Research [from Patrick Patterson and Paul Amato of the National Healthy Marriage Resource Center] shows that the after-effects on the family are traumatic and often chronic. Divorce seems to mark the end of a child's youth. Family break-up is extremely detrimental to children because children identify with the family rather than with the parents as individuals.

FAST FACT

According to the US 2009 Current Population Survey, only 38.1 percent of black children live in two-parent homes.

Compared to children from healthy, functional homes, children of divorce are far more likely to struggle academically, engage in drug and alcohol use and other high-risk behaviors, commit suicide, experience psychiatric problems, live in poverty, experiment sexually at earlier ages, and have a greater likelihood to divorce themselves. "The end result has been disposable marriages and shattered lives," [says United Families International].

After thirty years of study, many researchers conclude that divorce harms children in virtually every measure. Furthermore, numerous studies support marital longevity as a vital component of good health for children and adults alike. The research supports the common findings by mental health professionals that children suffer terribly in divorce, and many times the children's souls are basically ripped in half. Even as adults, children from divorced families are even less satisfied in their lives compared to adults from intact and happy families.

Factors Contributing to Divorce

The divorce rate began to rise in the mid-1960s due to the rebirth of feminism, new levels of social stress, cultural instability, sexual

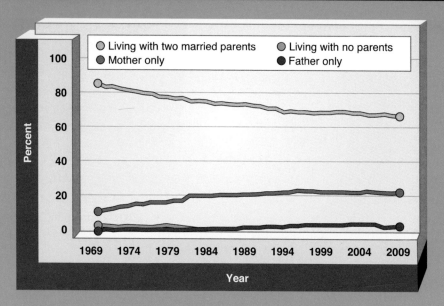

Living Arrangements of Children, 1970–2010

Taken from: Child Trends Data Bank. Available at www.childrensdatabank.org.

liberation, and the adoption of "no-fault" divorce. An often quoted article is "Making Marriage Last" [published in 2000 by the American Academy of Matrimonial Lawyers]. According to this article not all marriages fail for the same reason and the factors that seem to contribute the most include poor communication, financial problems, a lack of commitment to the marriage, a dramatic change in priorities, and infidelity. These factors together made marital stability more problematic, and divorce far easier.

For those who do advocate for divorce as a viable option, it needs to be stated that another social experiment has failed. Thirty years of study found that the decline of the two-parent, married-couple family results in poverty, educational failure, unhappiness, antisocial behavior, isolation, emotional problems, and social exclusion for thousands of women and men [according to an essay written by

Rebecca O'Neill and published by CIVITAS—The Institute for the Study of Civil Society, in 2002]. Especially affected, are the children of divorce—CODs.

A Real Social Malady

Research shows that: 63% of youth suicides are from fatherless homes; 90% of all runaway children are from fatherless homes; 85% of all children that exhibit behavioral disorders come from fatherless homes; 80% of rapes motivated with displaced anger are from men who come from fatherless homes; 71% of all high school dropouts come from fatherless homes; and 85% of all youths in prison are from fatherless homes. Other researchers found that the younger the child is at the time of the divorce the greater the impact. Note that, currently, nearly 2 of every 5 children in America do not live with their fathers [according to 2001 statistics from the organization Fathers for Life].

Divorce is also intergenerational. Children fail to successfully learn how to navigate through all the boundaries and obstacles of marriage. They learn that rather [than] cope, they can just opt out like mother or father did. This sets up a very negative cycle.

The family is a critical cornerstones of society, and healthy families bring strong stability and blessings to all society. Divorce is a reality and a necessity for some. The truth, though, is that divorce and the dissolution of families remains one of the strongest risk factors for children in America.

> ## EVALUATING THE AUTHOR'S ARGUMENTS:
>
> What are Acquilano's credentials in writing this viewpoint? Do you think he adequately supports his claim that divorce is extremely harmful to children? Why, or why not?

Divorce Can Be Good for Children

Jane Smiley

*"Divorce
. . . gave [my
daughter]
the tribe of
peers that
she wanted,
and she has
never seen a
downside."*

In the following viewpoint, Jane Smiley argues that divorce does not have to be bad for children. Smiley, whose parents divorced and who is herself divorced, contends that divorce can benefit children. For instance, she says, kids from divorced families get extended families, more than one "home," and the opportunity to learn more about love. According to Smiley, she is not praising divorce, but she does not think divorce is all that bad either.

Smiley is the author of numerous novels, including *The Age of Grief; A Thousand Acres,* which won the Pulitzer Prize in 1992; and the young adult novel *The Georges and the Jewels,* as well as many essays for such magazines as *Vogue,* the *New Yorker, Practical Horseman, Allure,* and others.

AS YOU READ, CONSIDER THE FOLLOWING QUESTIONS:

1. What response does Smiley say she received when she wrote an op-ed for the *New York Times* defending divorce?
2. What does the author say about the patterns of conflict that nuclear families tend to get into?
3. What does Smiley say she remembers reading about a crop of soldiers and junior officers in Iraq?

When I asked my older daughter what she thought of my divorce from her father (she is 32), she said, "Do you really think I wish we had remained in that suffocating little four-person family?" But my daughter is a pro-divorce radical. Even as a teenager, when she dated boys from nuclear families, she was open about how dull their lives were compared to ours—always the same few people sitting around after dinner, no step-brothers and sisters, half-brothers and sisters, foster brothers and sisters. Here we were with an extended family and none of the parents had had to defy the prescriptions of Zero Population Growth (she is strict about over-population). It was divorce that gave her the tribe of peers that she wanted, and she has never seen a downside.

I will say, though, that when I've defended divorce in the past—notably in an Op-Ed for the *New York Times*, the response has been outrage. In America, you are never supposed to treat divorce with anything but appalled lamentations. No type of family is better than an intact nuclear family, ever. That millions of Americans have voted with their feet for other types of families is just a sign of cultural failure, or personal failure (the personal failure of the divorced ones, of course—the married ones have at least kept it together, even if . . . well, I won't go into the cost of keeping it together. I come to bury divorce, not to praise it. Amen.)

Making Divorce Good for the Children

So, let me not praise divorce. Let me just offer a few suggestions about how to make it good for the children.

1. *No United Front.* People are quite frequently eccentric. Grown-ups quite frequently do not agree on basic issues like discipline of the children, the balance of power within the marriage, budgeting, running the household, sex, how the world works, etc. When they attempt to present a united front for the children, this can come to be, basically, a lie, as in "Daddy and I love each other very much, and we agree on everything, especially what is good for you." If the reality is that Daddy and I don't know what in the world we agree on or whether we actually love each other, then the dissonance between the presentation of the united front and what the child sees for him or herself can undermine the child's sense of reality. Once the parents are divorced, Mom and Dad are able to discuss with the children those

Divorce Can Be Best for Children

If parents are very unhappy with each other, are children better off if parents divorce or remain together?

2007 Survey of American Adults

It Depends
9%

Remain Married
19%

Get Divorced
67%

Taken from: *Pew Research Center.* "A Generation Gap in Values, Behaviors," July 2007.

things that they differ on. That doesn't mean either one can say, "Gee, your ___ is a full-fledged mindless jerk." A better approach: when the child says, "Why does ___ do that?", the parent says. "Well, here is how ___ sees it. Here are some reasons for that. It's possible to agree or disagree with that point of view, but I see it differently, and here's why." A steady diet of this, I think, allows the children not only to differentiate between the parents, but also to differentiate between lots of points of view, and to develop a point of view of his or her own. Most importantly, his or her sense of reality is not undermined by a determined effort on the part of the parents to deny reality.

2. *More Siblings.* I was an only child. I've known only children. From this experience, I do believe that the children should outnumber the parents. Parents are powerful. Children need friends and allies as

well as playmates and antagonists. They need a cohort of peers to liven the place up and counterbalance the parents' ideas. Combined families often get bad reviews, but the family my children got when they traded away "the suffocating four-person" nuclear one is one that has benefited all of them. My daughters got step-siblings with whom they have lifelong relationships and a half-brother they love, and my son got an older step-brother who has been an excellent example for him, and a good friend. The only siblings I have are half-siblings. My nuclear family would have been an extra-suffocating three-some. Instead, I have an interesting brother and sister, in-laws, and darling nephews.

Not everyone in my children's cohort has a relationship with everyone else, but the relationships that do exist are important to them. However, you must let these relationships form independently of you. You can't force the kids to like each other, though you can insist that they be courteous to one another and you can forbid bullying. And why shouldn't you? You wouldn't let them bully school friends, would you?

3. *Conflict Management.* It's good practice! Nuclear families tend to get into patterns of conflict that last for years and seem like normality. Step-families have to be more self-conscious about conflict management. My most important piece of advice is, the step-parent has to be the good cop and the parent has to be the bad cop, and both members of the couple have to do their jobs. This means that if there is some indulging to be done, the step-parent has to not only be willing to do it, but to do it sincerely. I mean, these are kids! They are not kids you gave birth to, but they are cute and they are inexperienced. They also can be won over with gifts and kindness. There is no reason to take a stand or operate by some authoritarian standard—as an intruder (in the eyes of the children), the step-parent does not have that option. If they behave badly, then the parent's job is to correct them, and the step-parent's job is to discuss this with the parent quietly and

reasonably behind closed doors when no one is angry. Forewarned is forearmed—the step-parent has to know going into the family that these conflicts will come up and have a strategy for not losing his/her temper and for persuading the parent to deal with things. The parent has to know that the children and the step-parent have to learn to like each other. Chances are that members of a couple with step-children had plenty of conflict in the marriages they have left, so now's the time to gain some self-knowledge and some new techniques.

Good Relationships and Home

4. *Love.* With luck, we learn more about love as we get more practice. Why divorce the father if we can't learn from it? I never saw an example of conjugal affection and compatibility until my mother married my step-father, and even though that marriage was cut short by his premature death eight years later, I knew what to emulate in my own adulthood. My partner and I offer a model of love that is kind, generous, affectionate, and fun. The children may or may not learn from it, but at least it is visible to them. Maybe, in fact, what it says to them is "if at first you don't succeed, try try again." Is that bad? I don't think so. I would be very sad if one of them got into a bad marriage and gave up.

5. *Home.* Everyone agrees that home is good and instability is bad. The nuclear family is supposed to offer a domestic haven in a scary world, and maybe it does. And maybe this haven is to be purchased at all costs—this is an individual decision. But any person or two people or three people can make a home, they just have to be willing to do it. When I was a child, my grandmother and grandfather made a part-time home for me, and now I would be sorry to have missed out on that, because they were vivid personalities and I loved them dearly. The home my mother made was appealing, too—she could cook and clean and decorate and welcome my friends. My two homes had two different sets of playmates and two different sets of activities. Because my mother was willing and able, I never felt strange in our two-person home, and because my grandparents were loving and involved, I never felt strange in their (our) home, either. My children were reared by joint custody—sleeping at each parent's house an equal amount of time. That they would feel at home in both houses

Nuclear families tend to get into patterns of conflict that last for years. Stepfamilies may be more aware of conflict management, the author contends.

was our first priority, and, according to them, they did feel at home, and also liked the change of venue. In fact, some of their friends were envious—two rooms? Two sets of Christmas presents? As I said, children are materialistic. The heart is where the home is, but you have to make it welcoming and homey. At the same time, children who have to negotiate two homes can learn to operate with flexibility and imagination. I remember reading in the *New York Times* that the crop of soldiers and junior officers in Iraq were cannier than their by-the-book superiors. This was attributed to what they had learned from divorce. I kid you not.

Divorce is based on the idea that we marry for love; you can't have one without the other. In cultures where marriage is based on property (women as property, marriage as exchange of property) divorce is much less common and love, at least for men, doesn't have to be (isn't often) a part of marriage (ask your wealthy French uncle if this isn't true). Falling in love is an expression of freedom and so is divorce. Freedom is, as they are always telling us, a responsibility. If we have the freedom to divorce, then we have to use it wisely. So far be it from me to praise divorce. For that, you're going to have to go to my daughter. Or [conservative, oft-divorced politician] Newt Gingrich.

EVALUATING THE AUTHOR'S ARGUMENTS:

Smiley and Nelson Acquilano, the author of the preceding viewpoint, offer different perspectives on the effects of divorce for children. What response do you think each author would have to the other's viewpoint? Is there anything you think the two authors might agree upon? What and why?

Teens' Relationships with Their Fathers Are Usually Harmed by Divorce

Tracy Kendricks

"The closeness between fathers and teens is harmed the most in a divorce."

In the following viewpoint, Tracy Kendricks asserts that divorced dads face challenges in staying close to their teenage children. Kendricks discusses research from Pennsylvania State University (Penn State) that found that the father-teen relationship declines after divorce. According to Kendricks, fathers are at a disadvantage to begin with, as they are typically not as comfortable as mothers in nurturing roles. Fathers are also the ones most likely to leave the home after a divorce, making it difficult for them to stay involved in their kids' lives.

Kendricks is a member of Divorce360 .com, a website that provides advice and community for people contemplating, going through, or recovering from divorce.

D ivorce can strain relationships for years. But a team of researchers at Penn State University has found that divorce impacts different family relationships in different ways. The closeness between fathers and teens is harmed the most in a divorce. Dr. Alan Booth, a professor of sociology and human development, co-authored the study. He found that divorced or not, there's a tendency for mothers to be more involved with children, especially teens. "Studies indicate that fathers are less involved . . . ," Dr. Booth reports. "We just don't have a heavy investment in the kids." As kids grow, they tend to grow "away"—toward peers, school and the world. "The relationship with the father declines normally, just in the natural course of things," Booth says, adding that when parents divorce, "fathers are more likely to let it slide."

David Vendig, 43, is an exception. It's been two years since the father of three children, (ages 13, 10, and 7), moved out of the Los Angeles home he shared with his ex-wife. And even though he moved just a few blocks away, it's not easy to parent post-divorce. Especially a teenager. "Finding alone time with any one of them takes planning and effort," Vendig says.

Another impediment is internal. "The other obstacle is self-doubt. Not knowing or believing that what I plan—or, if it's just hanging out— is good enough." Vendig's concerns are shared by many men. Dr. Booth says that's because mothers are more comfortable in the nurturing role.

Special Challenges

Whatever the circumstances, the Penn State study was clear: fathers and teens have a special set of challenges after divorce. The first is proximity. Dad is often the one who moves out, leaving the kids with the same schools, friends and address. But his time with the kids is cut down considerably. "It's just hard for dads to keep up," Dr. Booth found.

Also, Dad's new place is often not as comfortable—"I have a small apartment," Vendig says—and the kids aren't likely to feel at home. In order to maintain the closeness they had before divorce, most fathers will have to increase their involvement with their kids. And that's something the majority of fathers just don't do, the study shows.

Then there's bad blood. The conflicts that cause a couple to divorce aren't resolved when the marriage ends. And that can be a big obstacle to dads' maintaining relationships with their kids. Jane Reardon, a marriage and family therapist practicing in Los Angeles, says father-child relationships are vulnerable to anger between ex-spouses. "Mothers may find it impossible to contain the hurt rage they experience as a result of the change in their financial status and increased amount of responsibility for child-rearing," she says.

FAST FACT

According to 2007 data from the US Census Bureau, children live with their mothers in 82.6 percent of divorces involving children.

Long-Term Impacts

Many women retaliate by badmouthing the ex-spouse, which can poison the children against him. But mothers are not alone in dealing with the fallout of the breakup. Either party's emotional residue can cast a shadow on the post-divorce relationship with the kids. Vendig explains it well. "If I am not careful about the contact I have with their mother—meaning if I let myself get too close—my feelings of hurt and anger come up and it keeps me from being present with the kids."

Divorce can affect the kids often decades into the future. In Reardon's practice, she sees clients—adults in their 20s and 30s—who are still dealing with the aftermath of their parents' battles. "They now feel fragmented in their recollections," Reardon says, "and as adults have a harder time claiming their identity and forming sustained intimate relationships."

That's just one reason to resolve the issues that led to the divorce—which Penn State researchers found yields a number of dividends,

Researchers at Pennsylvania State University found that father-teen relationships decline after divorce because men are not natural nurturers. Moreover, the father is often not the primary caretaker, making it difficult for him to stay involved with his child.

chiefly, her cooperation and support. "If he keeps mom happy, she'll be less resistant," Dr. Booth says. Often a mother is the deciding factor in whether, how often, or how much kids see their dad. "If the mother is supportive, she'll push from her end," Booth says. Reardon sees the benefits: "My experience treating adult clients from divorced families shows a direct correlation between the continued involvement of both parents after the divorce, and the client's level of functioning."

New Relationships

A final obstacle pops up once the parents have moved on to a new relationship. As a psychologist, Reardon treats many children of divorced parents, now grown. She says her clients' biggest complaint, "is when either parent attempted to integrate their children too quickly into their new relationship."

While divorced dads may be eager to rebuild a family with the new partner, "teenagers are typically resistant to the plan," Reardon says. They often respond by exercising the only power they have—refusing to visit. "Single parents need to be very mindful of their own agendas in trying to blend new families too quickly," Reardon advises. "The comfort level of the children needs to take precedence over the accommodation of a new partner."

Dads need to take into account the length of time the family has been separated, as well as the length of the new relationship. Dr. Booth believes the new relationships "have a tendency to take time and energy away from the kids" and men need to make sure they choose a new partner who is open to children. "It's important that he select a woman who likes kids and isn't opposed to being involved with a child." If a new girlfriend opposes a man's children, Dr. Booth observes, "it's very difficult for the dad to maintain close contact with them."

The Penn State study did find some heartening news. For one thing, kids themselves can make a big difference in their relationship with their dad. "Kids have an effect on their fathers," Dr. Booth asserts. "If the kids want to maintain the relationship, they will." And that's something a dad can exert some control over. "It's important to stay at the front of your child's mind," urges Dr. Booth. "Call the

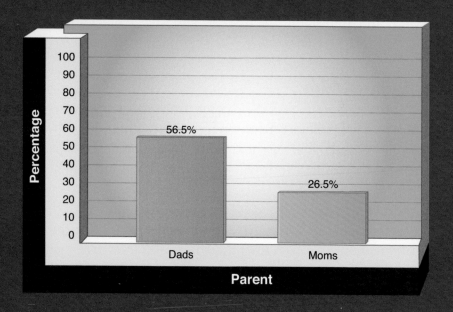

Teens Reporting a Decreased Relationship

Taken from: Mindy Scott, Alan Booth, Valerie King, and David Johnson. "Postdivorce Father-Adolescent Closeness." *Journal of Marriage and Family*, November 11, 2007.

child regularly, send letters, send gifts. Continuc to keep the child's attention, even though the child may be mad that dad left." It may take a while, even years, but Dr. Booth believes a father's actions over time do make an impression. "Eventually the child will see the dad differently, especially if the dad is really sincere."

Benefits of Staying Close

Last but not least, divorce, say Penn State researchers, can also have the surprising effect of actually strengthening a dad's relationship with his teens—something Vendig is finding out firsthand. "For me, processing this event has been a long growing process that includes stepping up as a father—probably more than anything else." In Vendig's experience the key to staying close to his son is to accept the process as just that—something that gets easier over time. He urges dads to go easy on themselves. "Be kind to yourself as guilt and shame are bound to come up," he says. "It will be messy at times, but surrendering to it all can bring freedom. As a father, and as a man."

EVALUATING THE AUTHOR'S ARGUMENTS:

Authors use several different types of evidence to support their viewpoints, such as personal experiences, expert opinions, statistical information, analogies, and examples. What types of evidence does Kendricks use to support her viewpoint? Do you think the evidence she provides is persuasive? Why, or why not? How would you make her viewpoint stronger?

Men Become Better Fathers After Divorce

Jill Brooke

"Many men become better parents post-divorce."

In the following viewpoint, Jill Brooke contends that divorce helps men become better fathers. According to Brooke, divorced fathers are required to perform many of the duties that mothers performed during the marriage, like making meals. These activities get them more involved in their children's lives. Brooke says divorced dads are finding creative ways to stay in their kids' lives, including using videoconferencing. In the past, says Brooke, divorced men tended to walk away from their wives and their kids; however, many men now realize that divorce does not mean they have to separate from their kids.

Brooke is a certified divorce coach, author of the book *Don't Let Death Ruin Your Life*, and a writer for the *Huffington Post* and FirstWivesWorld.com. Her work has also appeared in the *New York Times, Forbes, Chicago Tribune, Harper's Bazaar,* and several other publications.

AS YOU READ, CONSIDER THE FOLLOWING QUESTIONS:
  1. According to Brooke, courts are more willing to grant joint
     legal custody to fathers since a federal study showed what?
  2. What was the change from the 1970s to the 2000s in the
     percentage of nonresidential fathers who were involved with
     their kids, according to researcher Paul Amato, as cited by the
     author?
  3. What state laws does Brooke quote Gary Nicholson as saying
     are part of the problem facing divorced dads who want more
     time with their kids?

If divorce is in the future of duplicitous two-timers [former South
Carolina] Gov. Mark Sanford to reality TV's Jon Gosselin [a father
of eight], these men will have to navigate co-parenting. However,
a growing trend shows that many men become better parents post-
divorce, to the surprise of ex-wives who find it difficult to grasp that a
man who wasn't a good husband can indeed be a good father.

Take the example of Peter Giles. When Peter Giles' three daughters
were toddlers, work consumed him at the expense of family life. The
New York businessman would justify the absences as doing the right
thing for his family since he was providing the financial womb while
his wife was taking care of their other needs. What finally made him
a better father? Getting a divorce.

"The divorce was such a shock and forced me to take stock of who
I was and what success should look like," said Giles, whose ex-wife
Nancy Claus sought a divorce in 2001. "I came to realize that I had
been providing for my children but needed to be more to them."

Like the majority of divorcing men today, Giles sought joint legal
custody, which courts are more willing to grant since a federal study
shows that men paid child support 90 percent of the time [when they
had joint custody] in comparison to less than 45 percent when the
mother had sole custody.

Divorce Facilitates Involvement with Kids

When his daughters visited, Giles morphed into a multi-tasker taking on chores previously done by his wife, including cooking, buying

cosmetics and remembering to buy eggs and bacon at the market. "I wish he would have been as involved and helpful when we were married," said Claus. "But he has definitely become a much better Dad after our divorce." He is not alone.

"When a father is away from the stress of a failed marriage, he can be more relaxed and more reflective and as a result enjoy being more fully involved with his children," said Don Gordon, professor emeritus of psychology at Ohio University and the director of the Center for Divorce Education.

David Gestl, the divorced father of four in Stewartstown, Pennsylvania, agrees, adding how it's a relief not to argue about parenting styles which allows the father to develop his own. "In my marriage, I was always walking on eggshells and getting criticized," he said. "Recently after I made dinner, my son shook his chocolate milk and it went flying everywhere. I could say, just relax it's nothing a paper towel won't pick up. It's okay to make a mistake and fix it."

One benefit to divorce is that with scheduled rationed time, each parent doesn't take it for granted and can have more single-minded focus with their kids.

CNBC anchor Dennis Kneale says divorce has made him "vastly closer" to his 9-year-old daughter Jing-Jing. "In many families, mom is the center of everything and the husband is the supporting player," he observed. "But with divorce, I have had more one on one time with [my daughter] in ways I never did before."

In a study on non-residential fathers, researcher Paul Amato from Pennsylvania State University found that the percentage of non-residential fathers being involved with their children more than tripled from 8 percent in the 1970's to 26 percent in 2000's. A recent study by Kathleen Gerson, professor of sociology at New York University and author of *The Unfinished Revolution: How a New Generation Is Reshaping Family, Work and Gender in America* found the number to be 27 percent. "Large numbers of contemporary fathers are doing their best to fulfill their responsibilities as parents despite the limitations of not residing with their children," said Amato. "It's time to recognize, value and support the commitment of these men to their children."

Experts say that the rise of more involved fathers post-divorce is based on several factors that collectively aligned like shooting stars and is preventing what one organization calls "a parentdectomy." A kid-focus culture, for starters, has helped cement ties.

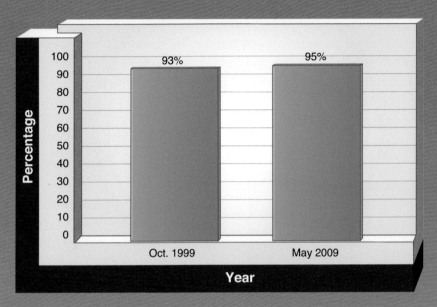

American Fathers Are Satisfied with Their Relationship with Their Children

Percentage

Oct. 1999 — 93%

May 2009 — 95%

Year

Taken from: 2009 National Fathering Survey. National Center for Fathering.

Dr. Warren Farrell points out that pop culture's parenting focus expanded the definition of a man's identity. In one study tracking data from 1965–1998, married men had doubled their direct child care involvement. "More men put in the effort early, which created deeper attachments that fathers didn't want to lose," said Farrell, who is also the author of *Father and Child Reunion*. Hence, more requests for joint custody.

Technology Helps Fathers Stay Connected

Technology has also helped prevent or reduce what is called parental alienation where in the past the residential parent may—consciously or unconsciously—block contact either out of her resentment towards the father or because she has remarried and is protecting the stepfather relationship. A study by J. Annette Vanini and Edward Nichols found that 77 percent of noncustodial fathers faced some form of visitation interference. But now fathers can give their kids pre-paid cell phones to insure contact. Divorce contracts are also often written to permit contact through email accounts.

Ted Rubin, a Huntington, Long Island, divorced dad to two girls, admits to using Facebook to keep in contact with his kids. "Sometimes when we speak on the phone I can tell if Mom is standing there and then later my daughter will contact me on Facebook," he said. "A lot of Dads complain that moms could stand in the way of communication but now it's almost impossible because kids are so tech savvy."

In fact, Rubin, who has a contentious divorce with his ex-wife, says that email helps divorced parents diminish "the nastiness is our dialogues" which the kids would overhear on the phone. Now he can email what time he's picking up the kids and delivering them without any verbal warfare.

Another big boost for continued contact has been videoconferencing. In 2002, Utah resident Michael Gough worried that his ex-wife's relocation to Wisconsin would wipe out his parental involvement. Considering that less than 10 percent of divorces go to trial, he fought to have the right to videoconference with his daughter. Utah was the first state to pass legislation for virtual visitation in 2004.

"It costs me thousands of extra dollars to go to court but as a result there is now a statute for videoconferencing that other judges and attorneys can refer to and follow," said Gough, who now runs a website called *internetvisitation.org*. Because of his efforts, Wisconsin, Florida and Texas all passed similar legislation and North Carolina did this month [July 2009].

"With videoconferencing, I was able to read bedtime stories, help her with her homework and even watch her open up a present," said Gough, with genuine sentimentality.

Schools are also helping divorced parents co-parent on neutral ground. While some wives would raise their eyebrows like thunderbolts when an ex-husband would arrive at the sports field, schools are not playing favorites.

"My ex-wife interpreted the divorce agreement that if I arrived at my son's soccer game that it should only be when I had him for an overnight," said Eric Ryerson, a nurse in Eugene, Oregon and father to an 11-year-old son. "But I want to see him more than my custody arrangement and by coming to sports events and volunteering at school, I can see him more."

Ryerson went to the school and volunteered to be a chaperone for class trips, signed his name to contact forms and also spoke to coaches to provide information on his son's soccer and baseball games.

"I asserted myself to be present and got rewarded for it," said Ryerson. "I also got to meet his classmates and interacted with them." Ryerson recalls fondly how in second grade he was nicknamed Mr. Pushy because he eagerly pushed his son's friends on the swings. "My son told me he liked it when I came to school."

Kids Like Having Both Parents Around

In fact, research shows that the kids do like it when both parents are present.

"They have fewer behavior and emotional problems, higher self-esteem and better school performance than children in sole custody arrangements," said Glenn Sacks, the National Executive Director of Fathers & Families. "When researchers have examined children of divorce, and studied and queried adult children of divorce, they've found that most prefer joint custody and shared parenting."

For example, in one Arizona State University study of college students who experienced their parents' divorces while they were children, over two-thirds believe that living equal times with each parent is the best arrangement. A Harvard University study also confirmed that children in joint custody settings fared much better than kids living in sole custody households.

While many men acknowledge progress, some still complain that the system treats fathers as second-class citizens when asking for more time with their children.

As Gary Nicholson, the president of the American Association of Marital Attorneys, explains, part of the problem is that various state laws tie child support payments to the amount of time a father is with their child. Payments can be adjusted if the father spends as much as

According to the author, divorce can help men become better fathers. Divorced fathers must learn to perform many duties formerly handled by mothers, such as making meals and supervising homework.

100 nights with his child so many mothers resist giving 50-50 splits and are angered by the request.

Said Nicholson, "Are there folks who look at this economically and think if I have equal time I won't have to pay as much child support? Yes. But the majority of dads want to he involved in their kid's lives. They feel they should be equal partners."

Loving Kids More than Hating Ex-Spouse

As the nation sees more divorced families, more parents have learned that even though the marriage is over, they are forever linked as co-parents. Cultural cues also encourage that they should love their children more than they hate their spouse. Over time, many hard feelings thaw and enhanced appreciation can ensue.

Deb Rabino, a New York based make-up artist, learned to admire her ex-husband's parenting of their two sons so much that when he lost his job in the financial industry, she voluntarily reduced his alimony and child support payments.

"He definitely became a better father after our divorce," she said. "He honored his support of us and now it was our turn to help him out."

The increased connection between children and fathers also results in other sacrifices as well. Michael Gough says videoconferencing helped get him more involved with his daughter. "My participation reminded me I have a daughter who needed me otherwise it could have been out of sight, out of mind." Because his wife later relocated to Austin, Texas, Gough now found a new job to be near his daughter.

"Videoconferencing really helped us stay closer," said Gough. "But it still can't replace seeing my daughter and getting a hug."

Like many men, he is getting remarried and may start a new family.

Love Is More Flexible than Most Think

As Stephanie Coontz, the Director of Research and Public Education at the Council on Contemporary Families, observes, men have for more than 150 years tended to think of the responsibility of kids as a package deal. When the relationship split up, they'd walk away and start new families. "But we're seeing a growing number of men separating from their wives but not their children," she said.

Do you have any doubt that recent divorced [celebrity] dads including Dylan McDermott, Robin Williams, Russell Simmons or Guy Ritchie won't enjoy time with their kids? All have said how much it means to them.

Still, it can be very painful for ex-wives to see that their families are living lives without them—especially when spouses repartner. However, in time, this divorce therapist has seen many women realize that a break from 24/7 parenting can benefit everyone. And love is far more elastic and flexible than we think.

EVALUATING THE AUTHOR'S ARGUMENTS:

What types of evidence does Brooke use to support her viewpoint? Compare the evidence Brooke uses to the evidence used by the author of the previous viewpoint, Tracy Kendricks. Whose evidence do you think is more persuasive and why?

Chapter 3

What Laws Should Govern Divorce Proceedings?

Divorce briefs are neatly stacked at a lawyer's office. Laws on divorce vary from state to state.

No-Fault Divorce Laws Are Not Beneficial

Beverly Willett

"If no-fault is good, why do we have the highest divorce rate of any Western nation?"

In the following viewpoint, Beverly Willett argues that no-fault divorce laws have not been beneficial to the partner unwilling to divorce. Willett details her unsuccessful fight to stay married to her husband and the father of her children. Her husband was eventually granted the divorce by moving to a no-fault divorce state. According to Willett, divorce is harmful, and making it easier is not fair to the spouse fighting to stay married and keep the family intact.

Willett is a writer and former entertainment attorney. She has written for the *New York Times, Newsweek,* and *Woman's Day,* among other publications.

AS YOU READ, CONSIDER THE FOLLOWING QUESTIONS:

1. According to Willett, by what year did every state except New York have a no-fault divorce law?
2. What no-fault divorce state did the author's husband move to in order to get a divorce?
3. According to Willett, what does no-fault divorce assume is the only reason parties would ever want to hold up a divorce?

My husband and I came from humble beginnings. We met in Manhattan in 1981 in the legal department of the company where we both worked. Having made it to New York from Southern Maryland, the last thing on my mind was marriage. But lo and behold, nine months later, we tied the knot. "Rest the security of your wedded life upon the great principle of self-sacrifice," my grandfather, the minister who married us, said—words I would never forget. Not even twenty years later when my husband wrongfully sued me for divorce.

Fighting to Stay Married

Over the years, our marriage saw more than its fair share of troubles. But we weathered the storms, and experienced miracles, too. In 1990, I gave birth to our first daughter. Five years later, healthy baby number two came along. My husband and I fell head-over-heels in love—with them. As his career began to blossom, I became a stay-at-home mom. Then one day, my husband began having an affair with a twice-divorced lawyer at his new job. A few months later, he left home for good, vowing to get remarried as soon as he got divorced from me. What he didn't realize was, we weren't getting a divorce. Not if I could help it.

I'm not sure my attorney thought I'd actually try and exercise my right to keep my family together. But that's what I did. In any other state it would have been impossible. But in 2003, New York was the last state in America that still didn't have no-fault divorce on the books. After California passed America's first no-fault law in 1970, divorce frenzy swept the nation, and by 1985, every state in the country had followed suit—every state except for New York, where my husband and I happened to live. When I refused a quickie divorce on his terms, he served me with divorce papers filled with baseless complaints. "The whole thing is a pack of lies," I said to [Saul,] my attorney, sobbing. "He's the one committing adultery." "Then deny it, and sue him for divorce," Saul said. "But I don't want a divorce," I cried. "I love my husband." Twenty years wasn't something I wanted to chuck overnight. Made of strong Southern female stock, I grew up believing the words "until death do us part" were non-negotiable. Family was paramount, and divorce virtually unheard of. "I don't think there's anything in life that can't be forgiven," my aunt said

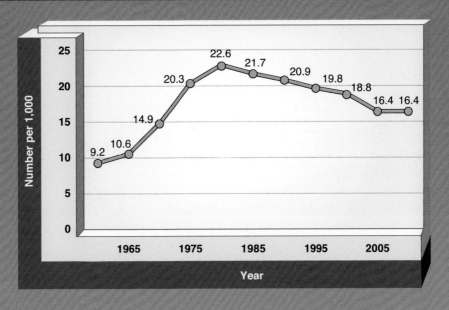

Number of Divorces per 1,000 Married Women Age Fifteen and Older, by Year, United States

Taken from: National Marriage Project. "When Marriage Disappears: The New Middle America." *The State of Our Unions,* December 2010.

when I asked for her advice. To me, that pretty much covered the whole territory.

One night when I was up reluctantly working on the divorce papers, my eldest daughter appeared by my side. "I don't want you to get a divorce," she said. I didn't either. Yet until this moment, it hadn't occurred to me that I had the power to stop this from happening. I realized perhaps the break-up of my marriage wasn't inevitable and that by standing up, maybe I could also help others.

While the law gave me the right to try to save my marriage, however, the deck was stacked against me. If parties didn't agree on a divorce in New York, the only way to exit a marriage was to prove the other spouse committed an actionable wrong like cruelty, sexual

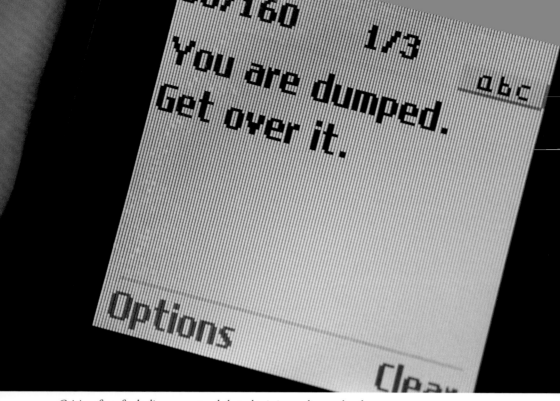

Critics of no-fault divorce contend that obtaining a divorce has become too easy.

abandonment, or adultery. But spouses wrongfully accused rarely exercised their right to fight. "Divorce is about money," Saul said. No one cared about right and wrong.

My husband said he'd fight me tooth and nail if I didn't give in. And there were times I nearly did. He kept a tight rein on the purse strings, said he'd seek sole custody, and had his lawyers pound me with paper. Crippling weight loss and the task of adjusting to life as a single mom nearly wore me to a nub. Nearly five years I fought to keep our bond from being broken.

On my first day in divorce court the judge peered at me over her spectacles and strongly recommended I stop being so stubborn. She gave me her "Exercise Your Rights, But It'll Cost You" speech, and made it clear that she'd prefer the case vanish from her docket. "Doesn't your husband have the right to move on with his life?" another judge wanted to know. My husband had broken his vows; the system simply assumed I wanted off the hook, too.

After a lengthy trial, the judge dismissed all of my husband's charges. But he was still determined. He moved across the Hudson River to New Jersey to establish residency. Within a year's time of living there, he would be allowed to sue me again under that state's no-fault law. Without the funds to keep fighting what was now the inevitable, I gave in. A year later, we had a second trial on financials, and our property was divided. When our divorce became final, my husband and I had been married for over a quarter of a century.

No-Fault Is Not the Answer

Last Sunday [August 22, 2010], I read that Governor [David] Paterson had signed a bill making New York the fiftieth and final state in the country to enact no-fault divorce. I was heartsick. We would never stand for arranged marriages, so why do we tolerate unilateral divorce, where the power rests in one person's hands to vote on behalf of the whole family? If no-fault is good, why do we have the highest divorce rate of any Western nation? Why is the divorce rate for second marriages even higher? Studies show most "unhappy" marriages ride out the storm. No-fault removes that option.

There are practical reasons against no-fault, too. Divorce reduces life-span. No-fault won't end litigation either, just shape-shift it as the litigation instead focuses on economics. And women and children are worse off financially after divorce, as they always have been, even those finally able to extricate themselves from domestic abuse.

Some say no-fault divorce would have been to my benefit. My legal bills might be less. But no-fault divorce takes away a woman's bargaining chips when her husband decides he wants to ditch her. No-fault assumes that removing choice from the equation will lead to less acrimony, but that's too simplistic. It assumes the only reason parties would ever hold up a divorce is to angle for money. It tosses aside the notion that one might want to stay married because of one's pledge, or for the sake of the children.

> ## FAST FACT
>
> In 1970 California became the first state to enact a no-fault divorce law. Forty years later, in 2010, New York became the fiftieth (and final) state to adopt such a law. The District of Columbia also has no-fault divorce.

Since 1970, approximately one million children a year have watched their parents divorce and their way of family life disappear. Children of divorce are more likely to divorce themselves, and divorce produces other negative consequences as well—more juvenile delinquency, aggression, teen pregnancy, depression, learning difficulties—not the least of which is the loss of childhood and parents and children losing precious time together. "The best interests of the child" governs in child custody, yet no-fault divorce does not serve that end.

The fact of the matter is that when couples have children you all become inextricably intertwined. I always pictured my husband and I turning to each other as we applauded our daughters in their school plays, and sitting in the car, tearful, after dropping our eldest off at college. It's nearly eight years since my husband left, and I still have trouble opening the family photo albums. But I've had to move on. There are more pressing problems like finding a job and health insurance when my costly COBRA [state-funded temporary insurance] runs out in about a year.

Governor Paterson commended New York's legislature for "fix[ing] a broken process." But no-fault isn't the answer. It won't cure our national preoccupation with searching for happiness in greener pastures—the root cause of rampant divorce—any more than a fault-based system of divorce can. We've created a happiness culture without understanding what that means or how to achieve it. Ditch your spouse and eat, pray, love your way to the next one.

"Stop trying to be Don Quixote [an impractical idealist]," my lawyer used to say. Now, with fault-based divorce eradicated in America once and for all, and no-fault the law of the land, standing up for marriage and family really is an impossible dream.

> **EVALUATING THE AUTHOR'S ARGUMENTS:**
>
> What effects do you think Willett's personal experience have on her viewpoint? Do you think her personal experience makes her viewpoint stronger or weaker? Explain.

Viewpoint 2

No-Fault Divorce Laws Have Both Positive and Negative Impacts

"Don't let anyone tell you it's obvious whether unilateral divorce laws are good or bad for you."

Betsey Stevenson

In the following viewpoint, Betsey Stevenson asserts that no-fault divorce laws have been both good and bad in different respects. In general, says Stevenson, no-fault divorce has provided positive benefits for women, such as reduced rates of domestic violence and suicide; however, Stevenson contends, no-fault divorce laws have also had adverse effects, including a weakening of the marriage commitment.

Stevenson is an assistant professor of business and public policy at the Wharton School at the University of Pennsylvania. She has written extensively on marriage, divorce, and families.

AS YOU READ, CONSIDER THE FOLLOWING QUESTIONS:
1. According to Stevenson, no-fault laws did more than just eliminate the need to demonstrate fault; they also allowed what?
2. What example does the author provide to show that no-fault divorce causes couples to invest less in their marriage in the early years?
3. What is the reason that Stevenson gives for the finding that women are more likely to be employed when divorce is unilaterally given?

Back in the 1950s, most states only granted "fault" divorces. In reality, this meant that when a couple wanted a divorce, they simply made up some marital fault, and the judge, with a nod and a wink, granted the divorce. Thus, if your spouse consented to the divorce, you could get one. . . . The divorce reform revolution changed all this. The new "no fault" laws did more than just eliminate the need to demonstrate fault. They also allowed you to unilaterally leave a marriage without demonstrating fault.

FAST FACT

New York became the last state to adopt no-fault divorce when Governor David Paterson signed the measure into law in August 2010.

New York was one of the few states to resist this change from consent-based to unilateral divorce.

My co-author Justin Wolfers [an economist at the Wharton School of the University of Pennsylvania] and I have studied the consequences of this change. The first conclusion is startling: changing divorce laws had little, if any, impact on the divorce rate. The divorce rate doubled between 1965 and 1975, but this happened in equal measure in those states adopting unilateral divorce, as in other states.

While New York's divorce laws bucked the national trend in the 1960s, its divorce rates did not. And so if New York eventually adopts unilateral divorce laws, we are unlikely to see much change in divorce rates.

Divorce Laws Impact Married Life

But divorce laws do affect marital life. In further research we uncovered evidence of a large decrease in domestic violence among states that adopted unilateral divorce laws, relative to those (like New York) which did not. This decrease was not just because abused women (and men) could more easily divorce their abusers, but also because potential abusers knew that they were more likely to be left. We found a 30 percent decline in domestic violence—an effect that could only occur if violence decreased in marriages that stayed together.

We also found that women were less likely to commit suicide when they were able to leave their marriages unilaterally. In short, we found that the adoption of these laws benefited the most vulnerable women substantially. New York can anticipate similar benefits if their no-fault divorce law passes. [It did.] . . .

Although no-fault divorce has led to a decline in domestic violence and suicide, critics say that it also causes a weakening of the marital commitment.

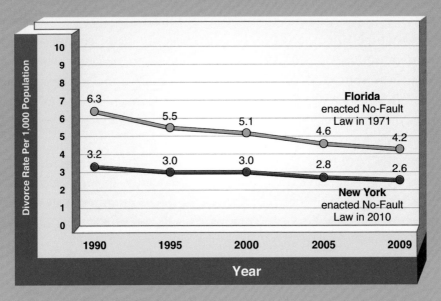

Divorce Rates in a Fault and No-Fault State

Divorce Rate Per 1,000 Population

Florida
enacted No-Fault
Law in 1971

6.3   5.5   5.1   4.6   4.2

New York
enacted No-Fault
Law in 2010

3.2   3.0   3.0   2.8   2.6

1990   1995   2000   2005   2009

Year

Taken from: US Centers for Disease Control and Prevention. National Vital Statistics System.

Not All Positive

But not all of the effects of changing divorce laws are positive. My research has also shown that couples invest less in their marriage in the early years when they face unilateral divorce laws. For example, spouses are less likely to support a spouse seeking further education.

Why is this? Well, with unilateral divorce laws it's hard to commit to not walking out of the marriage once your spouse has made a substantial investment in your career. Courts could help undo this effect by making sure that spouses share equally in all investments made during the marriage, including those involving human capital.

I also found women are more likely to be employed when divorce can be unilaterally granted. This is not because of a greater likelihood of being divorced and therefore needing to work (we've shown that there really isn't a greater likelihood of being divorced).

The reason is that unilateral divorce means that individuals have less control over whether they will stay married. Those who get left under unilateral divorce tend to be left worse off than if their spouse had to "bribe" them into consenting to lie about fault.

Women can protect against this risk by staying more attached to the labor force so that they are better able to support themselves in the wake of divorce. While today's women are more likely to work anyhow, it's likely that people will make other changes to help protect them in case of an unwanted divorce.

On balance, unilateral divorce favors those who most want out of the marriage, which more often than not are women. However, don't let anyone tell you it's obvious whether unilateral divorce laws are good or bad for you. It's hard to tell.

But I think that passage of reform will be a positive change for New York, particularly if policy makers consider the many ways that other aspects of divorce law can mitigate against the less positive consequences of unilateral grounds for divorce.

EVALUATING THE AUTHOR'S ARGUMENTS:

Stevenson is an assistant professor at the University of Pennsylvania. What impact do her credentials have on the strength of her viewpoint? What impact, in general, do you think scientific or academic credentials have on an author's viewpoint?

Viewpoint 3

Collaborative Divorce Proceedings Are Better for Children

"Collaborative Divorce can reduce the corrosive effect divorce may have on the children."

Michael McDonnell and Tiffany Moncrieff

In the following viewpoint, Michael McDonnell and Tiffany Moncrieff assert that a nonadversarial divorce proceeding, known as collaborative divorce, can reduce the negative impacts that divorce has on children. According to McDonnell and Moncrieff, traditional divorce proceedings, where spouses wage war on each other, can be emotionally devastating for children. Collaborative divorce, they contend, can reduce the negative impact, save money, and reduce the heartache of a divorce for all involved.

McDonnell and Moncrieff are Florida attorneys at a law firm specializing in collaborative divorce.

AS YOU READ, CONSIDER THE FOLLOWING QUESTIONS:
1. How does collaborative divorce differ from mediation, according to McDonnell and Moncrieff?
2. According to the authors, by definition, collaborative divorce requires what?
3. According to McDonnell and Moncrieff, under collaborative divorce, what happens if parents do not agree to a parenting plan?

It is a sad fact that intact marriages are eclipsed by the nearly half of all marriages that end in divorce; wounding the participants with enormous attorney fees, trauma to the children and damage to any hope of the couple retaining some measure of mutual respect. In the right situations the innovative process of "Collaborative Divorce" offers a chance to reduce such emotional and financial waste. It is a process through which the parties commit to reaching an out of court settlement without judicial intervention and differs from mediation in that the attorneys work jointly to make an informed recommendation as to how their clients should settle.

Problems with Traditional Divorce

Problems occur in the traditional divorce setting for multiple reasons, most of which might be best explained by mental health professionals. Uncontrollable anger, control issues, self destructive behavior and financial fears are primary contributors. Lack of insight into one's own behavior infuses the emotional landscape.

A significant tragedy is the impact of these struggles on the children. Florida law presumes that in "normal" cases children should have access to both parents since parents should exercise parental responsibilities fully and with due regard for the best interests

FAST FACT

The collaborative approach to family law was created by Minnesota attorney Stu Webb in 1990.

of the children. However, the emotional welfare of the children is oftentimes put at risk by those whose duty it is to protect and nurture it.

For a couple averaging $60,000 a year with at least one child and a home valued at $185,000, the average divorce costs are about $53,000.

Annual Income: $60,000	Divorce Cost: $53,000
Home Value: $185,000	Marriage therapy Child therapy Hire attorney Sell marital home Purchase another home Rent apartment

*Using 2006 US Statistics

Taken from: Divorce360.com. "Love Is Grand, but When It's Gone, Divorce Can Cost More than Twenty Grand," 2006. Available at www.divorce360.com/divorce-articles/finance/costs/divorce–100000.aspx?artid=1118.

In adversarial courtroom proceedings, spouses often come to the center of the ring and "beat" one another to an emotional and financial pulp. Attorney fees and costs can run fantastically high. Yet the results are frequently the same as if reason and common sense had been employed from the outset. "Bulldog" lawyers, considered by some to be the Golden Fleece [a magical solution] in these situations, may simply fuel negative emotions, run up bills and constitute part of the problem rather than the solution. As participants in mediation, such attorneys do so with polarized views, unrealistic expectations and perhaps more interest in ultimately preparing for trial. As William Shakespeare penned [in *Henry VI, Part I*], "Marriage is a matter of more worth than to be dealt with by attorneyship." The same can be said of divorce. Spouses invested in "revenge" are unable to observe when their hired guns fan the fires rather than dispel them. Responsible attorneys attempt to guide their clients in a productive manner, but the adversary process may blunt their efforts.

Nonadversarial Divorce

But hope exists in the Collaborative Divorce process. By definition, Collaborative Divorce requires a collaboration of efforts and an agreement from both parties and their attorneys to participate in a nonadversarial manner. However, some folks cannot muster the insight and self control that this new concept requires. The process begins with each spouse hiring Collaborative Divorce specialists who work together with their clients to reach a unified resolution. Each spouse retains their attorney's services with the understanding that if the process is unsuccessful, both attorneys must withdraw and cannot further represent the parties. This proviso keeps the attorneys focused on applying their knowledge of the law to reach a unified agreement, as opposed to "posturing" in preparation for trial.

Hopefully the attorneys ultimately develop a joint recommendation for settlement with their clients based on the law and facts. Of course neither client is obliged to follow that recommendation and may subsequently elect to hire alternate lawyers and revert to adversarial proceedings. However, if the clients follow their Collaborative

The most significant impact of traditional divorce is its effects on the children, whose parents may display uncontrollable anger and self-destructive behavior.

Divorce attorneys' recommendation, a written agreement is drafted, and a final judgment adopting the agreement and terminating the marriage is entered. The parties may save thousands of dollars in fees and hopefully a priceless amount of heartache.

The proper use of the process of Collaborative Divorce can reduce the corrosive effect divorce may have on the children. Parents are encouraged at the inception of their divorce to work together and see the benefits thereof. Parents frequently agree to a parenting plan. If not, specialists such as child psychologists may be consulted in formulating the children's and parent's rights with regard to parental responsibility. . . .

Collaboration could very well be one way for everyone to win in a losing situation. What great vision Helen Keller had in her belief that "Alone we can do so little; together we can do so much."

EVALUATING THE AUTHOR'S ARGUMENTS:

McDonnell and Moncrieff are attorneys at a law firm specializing in collaborative divorce. What influence might this have on their viewpoint? Does this fact affect your opinion of the validity of their viewpoint? Why, or why not?

Divorce Law Needs to Better Define the Best Interests of Children

"There are few cases anywhere in the country that even make an effort at defining 'best interests.'"

Gregg Herman

In the following viewpoint, Gregg Herman contends that when deciding child custody arrangements in divorce proceedings, the best interests of the children are the most important factor; however, Herman maintains, defining what the term *best interests* means has been difficult. For Herman, it means, generally, that shared custody is better than having parents fight over the children.

Herman is a family law attorney in Wisconsin. He has been editor in chief of the *Wisconsin Journal of Family Law* and has served on the board of governors of the State Bar of Wisconsin.

Winston Churchill once said, "There is nothing wrong with change, if it is in the right direction."

Over the past two decades, family law has seen tremendous change, mirroring changes in society. Years ago, for divorcing parents, the "child of tender years" doctrine meant that custody of minor children was usually awarded to the mother, with the father having visitation on alternative weekends and an evening or two during the week.

Today, legal custody is awarded jointly in virtually all cases, and physical placement is frequently shared equally. . . .

Any discussion of children in divorce has to start with the term "best interests."

> **FAST FACT**
>
> According to the US Census Bureau, in 2007 an estimated 13.7 million parents had custody of 21.8 million children under the age of twenty-one, while the other parent lived somewhere else.

Is there any legal term more used, but less defined? Indeed, there is no case in Wisconsin that even tries to define it. For that matter, there are few cases anywhere in the country that even make an effort at defining "best interests."

Rather, it is used as a lodestar, as an amorphous goal, rather than as a reality.

Indeed, a child psychologist once testified that the term could not properly be used. Since the "best" placement for children is to have one home and an intact family, she could not use the term "best" for a placement schedule for separated parents. In her view, the proper test should be which schedule would be the least detrimental alternative.

One Expert's Analysis

A number of years ago, as part of a select committee through the American Academy of Matrimonial Lawyers, I had the opportunity to discuss these issues with Judith Wallerstein, perhaps the leading researcher on the effects of divorce on children. Wallerstein's work includes *Second Chances: Men, Women and Children a Decade After Divorce, Surviving the Breakup: How Children And Parents Cope With Divorce* and *The Unexpected Legacy of Divorce: A 25-Year Landmark Study.*

When asked what factors were the most determinative of the effect of divorce on children, Dr. Wallerstein highlighted three:

1) Whether at least one parent (preferably, both) presents a warm, caring and loving environment;
2) The level of conflict between the parents; and,
3) The independent psychological makeup of the child.

It is generally accepted that child custody decisions should be made in the best interest of the child; however, just what those interests are has been difficult to define.

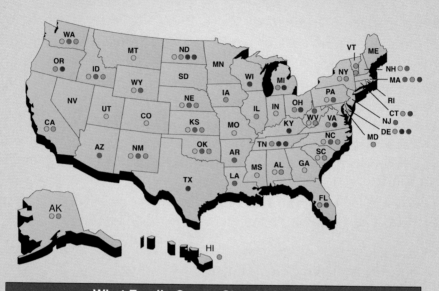

What Family Courts Should Consider:

- ○ Family Importance
- ● Health, Safety, and Protection of the Child
- ◐ Permanence
- ◑ Emotional Ties
- ● Domestic Violence
- ● All Relevant Factors

Taken from: US Department of Health and Human Services, March 2010.

As lawyers, there is little we can do about the first and the third of these factors. We can (and frequently do) refer clients to parenting classes to improve their skills, but otherwise, the legal system can do little at improving parenting ability. The DNA of the child was already selected.

There is a lot we can do, however, about the second factor; that is, to reduce the level of conflict.

To do so requires, as does much else in this area of law (and in life), a balancing test. When a parent wants an unequal placement schedule, the question is not whether such a schedule would be "best," but rather, would it be the least detrimental alternative. Included in that discussion has to be the possibility of a destructive battle over placement, substantially increasing the level of conflict involving the children.

Therefore, the balancing test is, how much does an extra day or two over a two-week period harm a child, compared to the harm of litigation? While there is certainly a positive attribute to stability, does the additional stability of an extra day or two merit the potential harm?

I don't have answers to these questions, which is my point. Likewise, mental-health professionals, social scientists or the trial courts also haven't concluded whether this particular change is in the right direction.

Therefore, the default position has become that, absent intervening circumstances, such as a history of violence or substance abuse, geographic difficulties or the entirely separate issue of teenage angst, the known harm to children by fighting over them is greater than allocating placement equally.

If anyone has a better analysis, please let me know.

> **EVALUATING THE AUTHOR'S ARGUMENTS:**
>
> What kind of evidence does Herman use to support his viewpoint? Do you think the evidence he provides is sufficient? Why, or why not?

Facts About Divorce

Editor's note: These facts can be used in reports or papers to reinforce or add credibility when making important points or claims.

Facts About Divorce and Men

According to the American Community Survey (ACS) data collected by the US Census Bureau for 2009, there were:
- 19.1 marriages,
- 9.2 divorces, and
- 3.5 instances of widowhood on average for every 1,000 men fifteen years and older in the United States.

The region with the highest divorce rates for men was the South. The divorce rate in the South for men was 10.2 per 1,000 men compared with:
- 7.2 per 1,000 men in the Northeast,
- 9.1 per 1,000 men in the Midwest, and
- 9.2 per 1,000 men in the West.

New Jersey had the lowest divorce rate for men (6.1 divorces per 1,000 men).

Arkansas had the highest divorce rate for men (13.5 divorces per 1,000 men).

The highest percentages of divorce occurred among men thirty-five to forty-four years old (29 percent).

For men who received their divorce in 2009:
- 18 percent were living with their own children,
- 16 percent were living with an unmarried partner,
- 5 percent were living in a multigenerational household,
- 15 percent were receiving public assistance,
- 17 percent had household income of less than $25,000,

- 33 percent had household income of more than $75,000,
- 11 percent were in poverty,
- 83 percent were working, and
- 57 percent owned a home.

According to the National Marriage Project's *The State of Our Unions: Marriage in America 2010*, in 2009, 9.2 percent of black males, 8.7 percent of white males, and 8.5 percent of males overall reported a marital status of "divorced."

Facts About Divorce and Women

According to the American Community Survey (ACS) data collected by the US Census Bureau for 2009, there were:
- 17.6 marriages,
- 9.7 divorces, and
- 7.8 instances of widowhood on average for every 1,000 women fifteen years and older in the United States.

The region with the highest divorce rates for women was the South. The divorce rate in the South for women was 11.1 per 1,000 women compared with:
- 7.5 per 1,000 women in the Northeast,
- 9.2 per 1,000 women in the Midwest, and
- 9.8 per 1,000 women in the West.

New Jersey had the lowest divorce rate for women (6.0 divorces per 1,000 women).

Alaska had the highest divorce rate for women (16.2 divorces per 1,000 women).

The highest percentages of divorce occurred among women thirty-five to forty-four years old (30 percent).

For women who received their divorce in 2009:
- 44 percent were living with their own children,
- 15 percent were living with an unmarried partner,
- 11 percent were living in a multigenerational household,

- 23 percent were receiving public assistance,
- 27 percent had household income of less than $25,000,
- 23 percent had household income of more than $75,000,
- 22 percent were in poverty,
- 81 percent were working, and
- 53 percent owned a home.

According to National Marriage Project's *The State of Our Unions: Marriage in America 2010,* in 2009, 11.8 percent of black females, 10.9 percent of white females, and 10.8 percent of females overall reported a marital status of "divorced."

Facts About Divorce and Children

According to the American Community Survey (ACS) data collected by the US Census Bureau:

Overall, 1,100,401 children, or 1.5 percent of children, in the United States lived in the home of a parent who divorced in 2009.

For children whose parents divorced in 2009:
- 64 percent were non-Hispanic white,
- 28 percent were living in a household below the poverty level,
- 53 percent were living in a rented home,
- 73 percent were living in households headed by their mothers, and
- 13 percent were living with a parent and that parent's unmarried partner.

Facts About the Risk of Divorce

According to National Marriage Project's *The State of Our Unions: Marriage in America 2010:*

An average couple who married in 2009 has a lifetime probability of divorce or separation somewhere between 40 to 50 percent. A person's risk of divorce decreases by
- 30 percent if he or she makes over $50,000 annually (versus under $25,000),
- 25 percent if he or she has graduated from college (versus not completing high school),

- 24 percent if he or she has a baby seven months or more after marriage (versus before marriage),
- 24 percent if he or she was over twenty-five years of age when married (versus under eighteen),
- 14 percent if he or she came from an intact family of origin (versus divorced parents), and
- 14 percent if he or she has a religious affiliation (versus none).

Organizations to Contact

The editors have compiled the following list of organizations concerned with the issues debated in this book. The descriptions are
derived from materials provided by the organizations. All have publications or information available for interested readers. The list was
compiled on the date of publication of the present volume; the information provided here may change. Be aware that many organizations
take several weeks or longer to respond to inquiries, so allow as much
time as possible for the receipt of requested materials.

Administration for Children and Families (ACF)
370 L'Enfant Promenade SW, Washington, DC 20447
website: www.acf.hhs.gov

The ACF is an agency within the US Department of Health and
Human Services. The ACF is responsible for federal programs that
promote the economic and social well-being of families, children,
individuals, and communities. The Office of Child Care and the
Office of Child Support Enforcement are primarily responsible for
child abuse prevention in collaboration with other ACF offices. The
ACF's Child Welfare Information Gateway provides many child
abuse and neglect prevention resources.

American Association for Marriage and Family Therapy (AAMFT)
112 S. Alfred St., Alexandria, VA 22314-3061
(703) 838-9808 • fax: (703) 838-9805
e-mail (online form): www.aamft.org/iMISpublic/Core/ContactUs
/ContactUs.aspx
website: www.aamft.org

The AAMFT is the professional association for marriage and family
therapists. The association works to increase understanding, research,
and education in the field of marriage and family therapy and to
ensure that the public's needs are met by trained practitioners. The

AAMFT provides individuals with the tools and resources they need to succeed as marriage and family therapists. The AAMFT hosts an annual national training conference each fall as well as a weeklong series of continuing education institutes in the summer and winter. The organization publishes the *Journal of Marital and Family Therapy* and the *Family Therapy Magazine* as well as a variety of brochures and pamphlets that inform the public about the field of marriage and family therapy.

American Coalition for Fathers and Children (ACFC)
1718 M St. NW, #187, Washington, DC 20036
(800) 978-3237
e-mail: info@acfc.org • website: http://acfc.org

The ACFC is a voice for "shared parenting" and is dedicated to the creation of a family law system and public awareness that promotes equal rights for all parties affected by issues of the modern family. ACFC challenges the current system of American family law and policy. The *Liberator,* ACFC's quarterly publication, provides a compilation of material from around the nation pertaining to family law reform.

Annie E. Casey Foundation
701 St. Paul St., Baltimore, MD 21202
(410) 547-6600 • fax: (410) 547-6624
e-mail: webmail@aecf.org • website: www.aecf.org

The Annie E. Casey Foundation, founded in honor of the mother of United Parcel Service (UPS) founder James E. Casey, is a private charitable organization dedicated to helping provide better futures for disadvantaged children in the United States. The primary mission of the foundation is to foster public policies, human-service reforms, and community supports that more effectively meet the needs of today's vulnerable children and families. In pursuit of this goal, the foundation makes grants that help states, cities, and neighborhoods fashion more innovative, cost-effective responses to these needs. The foundation provides many different publications, including the monthly magazine the *Urbanite* and the annual statistical report *Kids Count Data Book.*

Association of Divorce Financial Planners (ADFP)
514 Fourth St., East Northport, NY 11731
(888) 838-7773
e-mail: adfp@divorceandfinance.org
website: www.divorceandfinance.org

The mission of the ADFP is to heighten awareness of the benefits and the added value of divorce financial planning so that it becomes an integral part of the divorce process. The ADFP accomplishes its mission by developing outreach programs to financial professionals, allied divorce professionals, and the general public; providing continuing professional education and training opportunities for divorce financial planning practitioners; and participating in policy making regarding financial issues in divorce. The ADFP website provides a divorce handbook, divorce articles, and a blog.

Center for Marriage and Families at the Institute for American Values
1841 Broadway, Ste. 211, New York, NY 10023
(212) 246-3942
e-mail: info@americanvalues.org
website: http://familyscholars.org

The Center for Marriage and Families, based at the Institute for American Values, issues research briefs, fact sheets, and other material related to marriage, families, and children. FamilyScholars.org is the center's website, offering commentary from a wide range of bloggers as well as publications such as the annual report titled *The State of Our Unions,* which monitors the current health of marriage and family life in America. *The State of Our Unions* is produced in collaboration with the National Marriage Project at the University of Virginia.

Kids' Turn
1242 Market St., 2nd Fl.; San Francisco, CA 94102
(415) 777-9977 • fax: (415) 777-1577
e-mail: info@kidsturn.org • website: http://kidsturn.org

Kids' Turn is a nonprofit organization providing comprehensive programs for children and family members who are affected by familial separation. The mission of Kids' Turn includes helping children cope with parental separation, helping family members support their children, supporting the diversity of participants, and demystifying and destigmatizing the separation process. Kids' Turn promotes a healthy perspective and helps families understand that they are not alone. Kids' Turn provides educational programs and resources for children, adolescents, and parents experiencing separation or divorce.

National Council on Family Relations (NCFR)
1201 W. River Pkwy., Ste. 200, Minneapolis, MN 55454
(888) 781-9331
website: http://www.ncfr.org

The NCFR is an association of professionals dedicated to understanding and strengthening families. The NCFR's mission is to provide an educational forum for family researchers, educators, and practitioners to share in the development and dissemination of knowledge about families and family relationships; establish professional standards; and work to promote family well-being. The organization publishes three scholarly journals, the *Journal of Marriage and Family, Family Relations Interdisciplinary Journal of Applied Family Studies,* and the *Journal of Family Theory & Review.*

National Marriage Project at the University of Virginia (NMP)
PO Box 400766, Charlottesville, VA 22904-4766
(434) 321-8601 • fax: (434) 924-7028
e-mail: marriage@virginia.edu
website: www.virginia.edu/marriageproject

The NMP is a nonpartisan, interdisciplinary initiative at the University of Virginia. The project's mission is to provide research and analysis on the health of marriage in America, to analyze the social and cultural forces shaping contemporary marriage, and to identify strategies to increase marital quality and stability. The NMP, along with the Center for Marriage and Families at the Institute for American Values, publishes an annual report titled *The State of Our Unions,* which monitors the current health of marriage and family life in America.

National Organization for Women Foundation (NOW Foundation)
PO Box 1848, Merrifield, VA 22116-1848
(202) 628-8669
website: www.nowfoundation.org

The NOW Foundation is a nonprofit organization devoted to furthering women's rights through education and litigation. The NOW Foundation is affiliated with the National Organization for Women (NOW), the largest women's rights organization in the United States. NOW supports no-fault divorce laws; works to eliminate discrimination and harassment in the workplace, schools, the justice system, and all other sectors of society; fights to secure abortion, birth control, and reproductive rights for all women; advocates to end all forms of violence against women; labors to eradicate racism, sexism, and homophobia; and works to promote equality and justice in society. The newsletter from the NOW Family Law Committee focuses on the issues women and children face in family courts.

Books

Barash, Susan Shapiro. *Women of Divorce: Mothers, Daughters, Stepmothers: The New Triangle.* Far Hill, NJ: New Horizon, 2002. This book offers divorce advice for the new triangle of mothers, daughters, and stepmothers that is created during the divorce process. Advice is offered on everything from how a parent's remarriage changes his or her daughter's personal universe to how to forge new bonds with a stepparent and step siblings.

Cassella, Lynn, and Father Theodore Hesburgh. *Making Your Way After Your Parents' Divorce: A Supportive Guide for Personal Growth.* Liguori, MO: Liguori, 2002. Written by a child of divorce and a Catholic priest, this book examines the effects of divorce on children during their growing-up years. Advice covers topics such as denial, shame, guilt, grief, anger, and rejection.

Cherlin, Andrew. *The Marriage Go Round: The State of Marriage and the Family in America Today.* New York: Random House, 2009. Johns Hopkins University sociologist Cherlin analyzes the changes that have occurred in family life since the middle of the twentieth century. His book compares marriage and divorce in the United States with other Western countries and finds that Americans have the highest levels of moving from partner to partner. According to Cherlin, this illustrates the tension between the American cultural ideal of commitment to marriage and the appeal of individual freedom.

Chesler, Phyllis. *Mothers on Trial: The Battle for Children and Custody.* 2nd ed. Chicago: Lawrence Hill, 2011. This book draws upon case studies, empirical data, and historical information to examine the treatment of mothers by the US justice system. Chesler says that mothers are measured against a mythological ideal that is hard to measure up to. Fathers, on the other hand, are given the benefit of the doubt. According to Chesler, in many cases fathers who have neglected, molested, kidnapped, beaten, and brainwashed their children have been awarded custody over mothers who have for years been the children's sole caretakers and nurturers.

Coles, Roberta, and Charles Green, eds. *The Myth of the Missing Black Father*. New York: Columbia University Press, 2009. This volume examines black fatherhood in America. According to the editors, common stereotypes portray black fathers as being largely absent from their families. However, while black fathers are less likely than white and Hispanic fathers to marry their child's mother, many continue to find ways of supporting their families.

Housden, Maria. *Unraveled: The True Story of a Woman Who Dared to Become a Different Kind of Mother*. New York: Harmony, 2005. This is a personal story about a woman who challenges conventional thinking about marriage, mothering, and family. After losing her young daughter to cancer, Housden divorces her husband and becomes a part-time mom to her three surviving children. Inspired by her dying daughter to live life to the fullest, she ventures out on her own in search of a more meaningful life. Despite criticism and disbelief from her friends and family, Housden finds happiness and experiences a deeper and more loving connection with her surviving children.

Krafsky, K. Jason, and Kelli Krafsky. *Facebook and Your Marriage*. Maple Valley, WA: Turn the Tide Resource Group, 2010. This book, written by a married couple, is a guide on how to use Facebook without putting your marriage at risk. The book provides answers, tips, and insights for how to use Facebook, protect your marriage, enhance your relationship, and deal with the many issues and situations that can come up on the world's most popular online social network.

Neustein, Amy, and Michael Lesher. *Madness to Mutiny: Why Mothers Are Running from the Family Courts—and What Can Be Done About It*. Holliston, MA: Northeastern University Press, 2005. This book provides an examination of the US family court system by a sociologist and a family attorney. According to the authors, the family court system is seriously dysfunctional and fails to protect the people the system is designed to protect. Specifically, the authors chronicle cases in which mothers who believe their children have been sexually abused by their fathers are disbelieved, ridiculed, or punished for trying to protect them.

Scarf, Maggie, *Intimate Worlds: How Families Thrive and Why They Fail.* New York: Ballantine, 2010. This book explores the factors that go into the formation and functioning of a family. Five different families representing a continuum from an optimally functioning family to a dysfunctional family are analyzed. Within these five families, the author explores such topics as the nature of human love, nurturance, sexuality, and the conscious and unconscious aspects of a family's world.

Unger, Donald. *Men Can: The Changing Image and Reality of Fatherhood in America.* Philadelphia: Temple University Press, 2010. In this book, a teacher and a father uses his personal experiences, stories of real-life families, as well as representations of fathers in the media to illuminate the role of men in America. The author tells the stories of a half-dozen families of varied ethnicities, geographical locations, and philosophical orientations in which fathers are either primary or equally sharing parents.

Wilcox, W. Bradford. *Why Marriage Matters: Twenty-Six Conclusions from the Social Sciences.* 3rd ed. Poulsbo, WA: Broadway, 2011. Led by the author, who is director of the National Marriage Project, a group of eighteen family scholars offer up-to-date findings from the social sciences on the state of marriage in the United States. Among the major findings discussed by the scholars is that while divorce rates for families with children have fallen, family instability continues to increase for the nation's children overall, in part because more than 40 percent of American children will now spend time in a cohabiting household.

Wilson, James. *The Marriage Problem: How Our Culture Has Weakened Families.* HarperPaperbacks, 2003. A detailed study on how American culture has weakened the family bond and the ability to resist divorce. The two sides of today's American family are examined—one consisting of parents, safe homes, and good education and the other where children are raised by only one parent in poor neighborhoods with high rates of crime. This study reveals that these two sides come about due to the effects of divorce on children and families.

Periodicals and Internet Sources

Barr, Katherine. "When Parents of Children with Special Needs Divorce," *Exceptional Parent,* February, 2010.

Coontz, Stephanie. "Divorce, No-Fault Style, *New York Times,* June 16, 2010.

Crain's New York Business, "Gray Divorce; Adult Children Take It Hard When Parents Split," April 24, 2006.

Economist, "I Do (Conditions Apply)," August 6, 2011.

Engemann, Kristie M., and Michael T. Owyang. "Splitsville: The Economics of Unilateral Divorce," *Regional Economist,* January, 2008.

Ferrari, Paige. "Untying the Knot," *New York Times Magazine,* September 11, 2011.

FitzGerald, Eileen. "Siblings Aim to Change Child Custody Law," Newstimes.com, October 10, 2010. www.newstimes.com.

Gildin, Steven. "What About the Kids? Getting a Divorce Without Hurting Your Children," *Going Bonkers Magazine,* Winter 2009.

Hetter, Katia. "What's Fueling Bible Belt Divorces," CNN Living, August 25, 2011. http://articles.cnn.com.

Hoffman, David A. "Divorce Is Costly. The Settlement Need Not Be," *Christian Science Monitor,* July 30, 2010.

Hughes, Robert. "How Religion Shapes Our Attitudes Toward Divorce," *Huffington Post,* November 15, 2010.

Jayson, Sharon. "Report: Cohabiting Has Little Effect on Marriage Success," *USA Today,* October 14, 2010.

Jefferson, David. "The Divorce Generation Grows Up," *Newsweek,* April 21, 2008.

Jenkins, Kathleen E. "In Concert and Alone: Divorce and Congregational Experience," *Journal for the Scientific Study of Religion,*" June 2010.

Jeynes, William. "The Two-Biological-Parent Family and Economic Prosperity: Where to Go from Here," *Public Discourse: Ethics, Law and the Common Good,* July 22, 2011.

Kershaw, Sarah. "Now, the Bad News on Teenage Marriage," *New York Times,* September 3, 2008.

Lee, Amy. "Recession Divorce Rates: Marital Unions Unraveling as Economy Bounces Back?," *Huffington Post*, February 11, 2011.

O'Neill, Rebecca. "Experiments in Living: The Fatherless Family," *Civitas*, September 2002.

Setoodeh, Ramin. "My Favorite Mistake," *Newsweek*, August 15, 2011.

Smith, Mark A. "Religion, Divorce, and the Missing Culture War in America," *Political Science Quarterly*, Spring 2010.

Stout, Hilary. "Why Does Manimony Feel So Wrong?," *Marie Claire*, May 2011.

Sultan, Aisha. "For Live-in Lovers, Breaking Up Can Be Worse than a Divorce," *St. Louis Post-Dispatch*, March 20, 2011.

Tavernise, Sabrina, and Robert Gebeloff. "Once Rare in Rural America, Divorce Is Changing the Face of Its Families," *New York Times*, March 23, 2011.

Websites

Fathers and Families (www.fathersandfamilies.org). Provides information about and advocates for fathers, shared parenting, and family court reform.

National Center on African American Marriages and Parenting (www.hamptonu.edu/ncaamp). Provides information to encourage, support, and help revive African American marriages and other family relationships.

Pew Research Center's Social and Demographic Trends (http://pewsocialtrends.org). Provides information about marriage, family relationships, divorce, lifestyle, and socioeconomic topics among other social and demographic issues.

US Census Bureau (www.census.gov/population/www/socdemo/hh-fam.html). Provides statistics about families and living arrangements from the 2010 US Census.

Index

Facebook is not increasing, 26–30
in fault *vs.* no-fault states, *104*
is dropping, 18–19, 27, 60
by religious affiliation, *44*
state of economy and, 7–9
states with highest/lowest, *14*
trends in, *19, 97*
Divorcerate.org (website), 36
Donohue, Elisabeth, 54, 56
Drake, Perry, 30

E
Economic costs
of divorce to families, 7, 54, *108*
of high divorce rates, 56
Economic Policy Institute, 8
Edin, Kathryn, 64
Education
impact on views of marriage/divorce, 63–64
out-of-wedlock births and level of, 63
wages/employment rates and, 65
Ephron, Nora, 32, 33

F
Facebook
average number of friends per user, 29
is increasing divorce rates, 21–25
is not increasing divorce rates, 26–30

numbers of users, *28*
percentage of US population with account on, 22
Falwell, Jerry, 42, *43*
Families, programs to strengthen, 56–58
Farrell, Warren, 89
Fathers
after divorce men become better, 86–93
divorced, relationships with their children, 89
divorce harms teens' relationships with, 79–85
percentage of children living without biological, 90
proportion of children not living with, 71

G
General Social Survey, 62, 64
Georgia College and State University, 56
Gerson, Kathleen, 88
Gestl, David, 88
Giles, Peter, 87–88
Gini, Marianna, 25
Gordon, Don, 88
Gough, Michael, 90, 93
Great Depression, 8, 9
Great Recession (2007–2009), 8
Gregoire, Christina, 35

H
Haskins, Ron, 54, 56
Hassett, Kevin, 53

Healthy Marriage Initiative, 56
Henry VI, Part I (Shakespeare), 108
Herman, Gregg, 111

I
Institute for the Study of Civil Society (CIVITAS), 71

K
Kaiser Family Foundation, 66
Keenan, Mark, 29–30
Kefalas, Maria, 64
Kendricks, Tracy, 79
Kneale, Dennis, 88

L
Leave It to Beaver (TV program), 32, *33*
Levinger, George, 29
Lloyd, Dorothy, 18
Lorber, Scott, 32

M
Marriage
   first, rise in average age at, 60–61
   impacts of no-fault divorce laws on, 103–104
   levels of happiness in, 60, 62
   percentage ending in divorce, 54
   probability break up by importance of religion and duration of, *50*
   soul-mate model of, 64–65
Marriage counseling, 14–15

Marriage rate(s), 17, 18
   is dropping, 27
Martin, Steven, 62
McDonnell, Michael, 106
McLanahan, Sara, 54, 56
Medical insurance, 37
Mohler, R. Albert, Jr., 40
Moncrieff, Tiffany, 106
Moral Majority, 42

N
National Center for Health Statistics (NCHS), 27
National Fatherhood Initiative, 63, 90
National Marriage Project (University of Virginia), 8
NCHS (National Center for Health Statistics), 27
Nichols, Edward, 89
Nicholson, Gary, 91, 92
No-fault divorce laws
   are not beneficial, 95–100
   first state with, 99
   have both positive/negative impacts, 101–105

O
O'Neill, Rebecca, 71
Opinion polls. *See* Surveys
Out-of-wedlock births, 63

P
Patel, Emma, 22
Paterson, David, 99, 100, 102
Patterson, Patrick, 69
Pensions, 38

Pew Research Center, 29
Picket, Sarah, 25
Polls. *See* Surveys
Poverty, 8
    child, role of family
       breakdown in, 66, 69
    decline in two-parent
       households contributes to,
       70
    as factor in divorce, 64

R
Rabino, Deb, 92
Reardon, Jane, 81, 83
Religion, impact on divorce,
    49. *50*
Rubin, Ted, 90
Ryerson, Eric, 91

S
Sacks, Glenn, 91
Sales, Wendy, 32
Same-sex marriage, 12,
    44–45
Scafidi, Ben, 66
Schlesinger, Richard, 31
Shakespeare, William, 108
Smiley, Jane, 72
Smith, Mark A., 41, 43, 44
Social Media Today (website), 22
Social networking, usage of, by
    country, *24*
Social Security, 38
Spencer, Lyle M., 7
Stanley, Scott, 49
Stanton, Glenn T., 46
States

adoption of no-fault divorce
    laws in, 96, 99
costs of family fragmentation
    to, *57*
definition of "best interests"
    of child in, *114*
fault *vs.* no-fault, divorce
    rates in, *104*
with highest/lowest divorce
    rates, *14*
Stepfamilies Foundation, 75
Stevenson, Betsey, 19, 101
Stouffer, Samuel A., 7
Surveys
    on joint custody, 91
    on parents staying together
       vs. divorcing, 63, *74*
    on relationship status of
       Americans 45 years and
       older, *37*
    on tightening divorce laws, 64

T
TANF (Temporary Assistance
    for Needy Families), 56
Taylor, Amy, 25
Technology, helps fathers stay
    connected with children,
    89–90
Teenagers. *See* Children/
    adolescents
Temporary Assistance for
    Needy Families (TANF), 56

U
Unemployment, 8
    education and, 65

Picture Credits

© aberCPC/Alamy, 23

AP Images/Mark Humphrey, 43

© Stuart Aylmer/Alamy, 98

© David Barrett/Alamy, 17

© Robin Beckham/BEEPstock/Alamy, 68

© Bubbles Photolibrary/Alamy, 55, 77, 92

BURGER/PHANIE/Photo Researchers, Inc., 52

© Catchlight Visual Services/Alamy, 103

CBS/Landov, 33

© Bernhard Classen/Alamy, 13

Joe Corrigan/Getty Images for AOL, 27

© Oredia Eurl/SuperStock, 82

© Owen Franken/Alamy, 94

Gale/Cengage Learning, 14, 19, 24, 28, 34, 37, 44, 50, 57, 65, 70, 74, 84, 89, 97, 104, 108, 114

© Angela Hampton Picture Library/Alamy, 38

Phillip Hayson/Photo Researchers, Inc., 10

© PhotoAlto/Alamy, 113

Spencer Platt/Getty Images, 63

© Don Smith/Alamy, 109

© SuperStock/Alamy, 48

© WoodyStock/Alamy